STEPHEN BIESTY'S
INCREDIBLE
EVERYTHING

ILLUSTRATED BY
STEPHEN BIESTY

WRITTEN BY
RICHARD PLATT

G^E

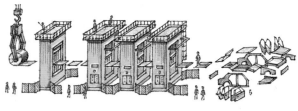

G^E

Senior Art Editor Dorian Spencer Davies
Senior Editor John C. Miles
Deputy Art Director Miranda Kennedy
Deputy Editorial Director Sophie Mitchell
Production Charlotte Traill
DTP Designer Karen Nettelfield

First published in 1997
by Dorling Kindersley Limited,
9 Henrietta Street, London WC2E 8PS
This edition published in 2000 for Greenwich Editions

A member of the Chrysalis Group plc

Illustrations copyright © 1997 Stephen Biesty
Text copyright © 1997 Richard Platt
Compilation copyright © 1997 Dorling Kindersley Limited, London

A CIP catalogue record for this book is available
from the British Library

ISBN 0 8628 8377 6

Reproduced by Dot Gradations, Essex
Printed ad bound in Spain by Artes Gráficas Toledo S.A.U.
D.L. TO: 1438-2000

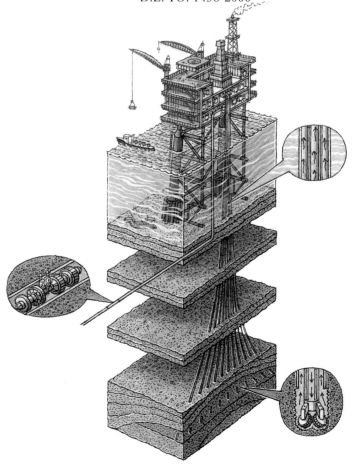

CONTENTS

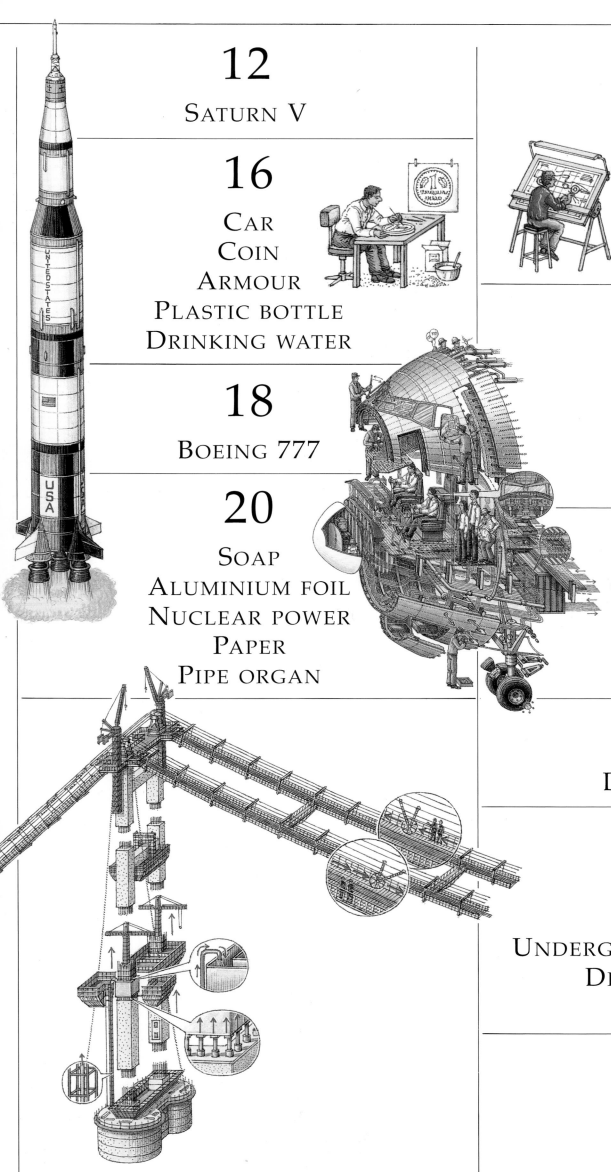

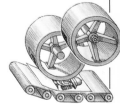

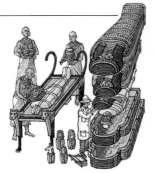

OUR INCREDIBLE WORLD

"HELLO! I'M CHESTER THE TESTER. Stephen Biesty has asked me to help him find out how all sorts of fascinating things are made. Some are everyday objects such as a newspaper, others are amazing creations, like a rocket that can take humans to the Moon. Checking everything thoroughly is serious work – do you have any idea how much testing needs to be done in a chocolate factory? But my assistant, Hector the inspector, is going to help – so look out for us at work."

"Chester, would you mind testing my sandwiches. I'm not sure which are the peanut butter and jelly ones!"

Tower block

"Now, let's see how fast this monster can move."

Model dinosaur

"Aiieee – careful! These swords are really sharp."

Armour

Racing car

"This string seems strong enough to me."

Nuclear power station

Plywood

"Have you seen my mummy?"

Gunpowder

"The gunpowder testing is very noisy so I'm wearing my earplugs."

"Incredible! The cannon still works after all these years."

Steam locomotive

"I wonder what happens here?"

Gas

"It's not often I get to travel in this manner!"

Drinking water

Underground railway tunnel

Newspaper

Bric

"This beats the crush inside."

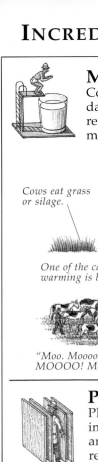

MILK

Cows are milked twice a day, but robots will soon replace manually operated milking machines.

The farmer takes a sample before milking.

The farmer and tanker driver agree on how much milk has been collected.

Pump

Driver smells milk

4. A tanker collects the day's milk. The driver smells it before pumping it up.

5. A weighbridge (drive on scale) at the dairy measures the weight of the tanker, to check the quantity of milk.

The tanker drives on full...

...and drives off unloaded.

Cows eat grass or silage.

They drink 60 litres (13 gallons) of water a day.

One of the causes of global warming is bovine flatulence.

"Moo. Moooo! MOOOO! Pthrpppt! Moo! MOOOO! Moooo! Pthrpppt! MOOOO!"

A tank in the barn holds the fresh milk.

Chilled storage tank

1. Food entices the cow into the milking parlour, where the dairy hand cleans the animal's udder.

2. Pulses of suction hold the milking cups on the udder. The cow feels as though a calf is suckling, stimulating milk flow.

3. A pump channels the milk from all the cows into a chilled tank. Stirring stops the cream from separating.

Milk is pumped to the dairy's bulk reservoir.

PLYWOOD

Plywood gets its immense strength and water resistance from veneers (thin sheets of timber) which are held together with synthetic glues. Early plywoods used glues made of blood, or the bones, horns, and feet of animals.

Long logs are debarked and cut into small lengths of wood.

Saw

1. Debarking and soaking prepares logs for plywood production. Then a saw cuts the wood into pieces of equal length.

A worker loads the log into the peeling machine.

Soaking the logs in hot water softens them.

A sharp blade peels away pieces of veneer.

3. Passing the veneer through a continuous heated tunnel dries the wood. Clippers cut it into sheets.

4. Graders select the best veneer for the face (front) of the plywood. Second-best goes on the back, and poor quality wood forms the core.

2. A lathe turns the log against a fixed blade, to peel off strips of veneer. Workers roll the veneer onto a spindle.

Spindle

Workers grade veneer sheets

Heated tunnel

5. Workers remove defects and knots, and fill in the holes. Gluing sheets edge-to-edge creates large panels of equal size.

Stacking veneer

6. Veneer that will be used to form the core is coated with glue on both sides. Glued panels are sandwiched between unglued sheets.

After the flaws are removed, workers fill the holes with circles of veneer.

Workers cut out knots and flaws in the veneer sheets.

Face

Huge hydraulic rams squash the plywood.

"Two plywood sandwiches, please!"

Unglued core sheets

Glued core sheets

Steam heats the press.

Back

Modern synthetic glues are stronger than the wood itself.

Wood splits easily along the grain, but has great strength across it. Plywood is strong because the grain direction crosses on alternate layers.

7. The final stage in manufacture is to bond the plywood together. A gigantic press squeezes and heats stacks of assembled veneer "sandwiches".

Finished sheets are removed from the press and stacked.

WOODEN HOUSE

Many houses built since about 1835 are constructed using a lightweight frame, with strips of thin timber in place of the heavy timbers used in older houses.

Damp-proof course

1. The house stands on solid foundations made by digging trenches and filling them with concrete. A damp-proof course (a strip of waterproof material) keeps the wall above it dry.

On houses such as this one, the finished frame is clad with wood. Other houses may have brick or flat pieces of stone as cladding.

The carpenters' fashion for exposing thin wooden supports led people to nickname homes like these "stick-style" houses.

This style of wooden house became fashionable as cities spread out into suburbs a century ago.

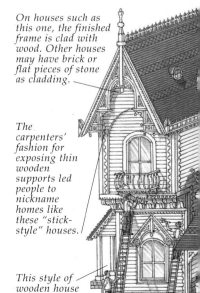

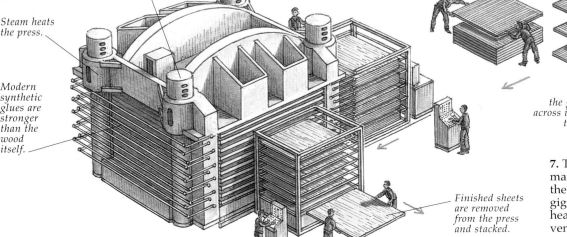

Details such as this gable trim are made elsewhere.

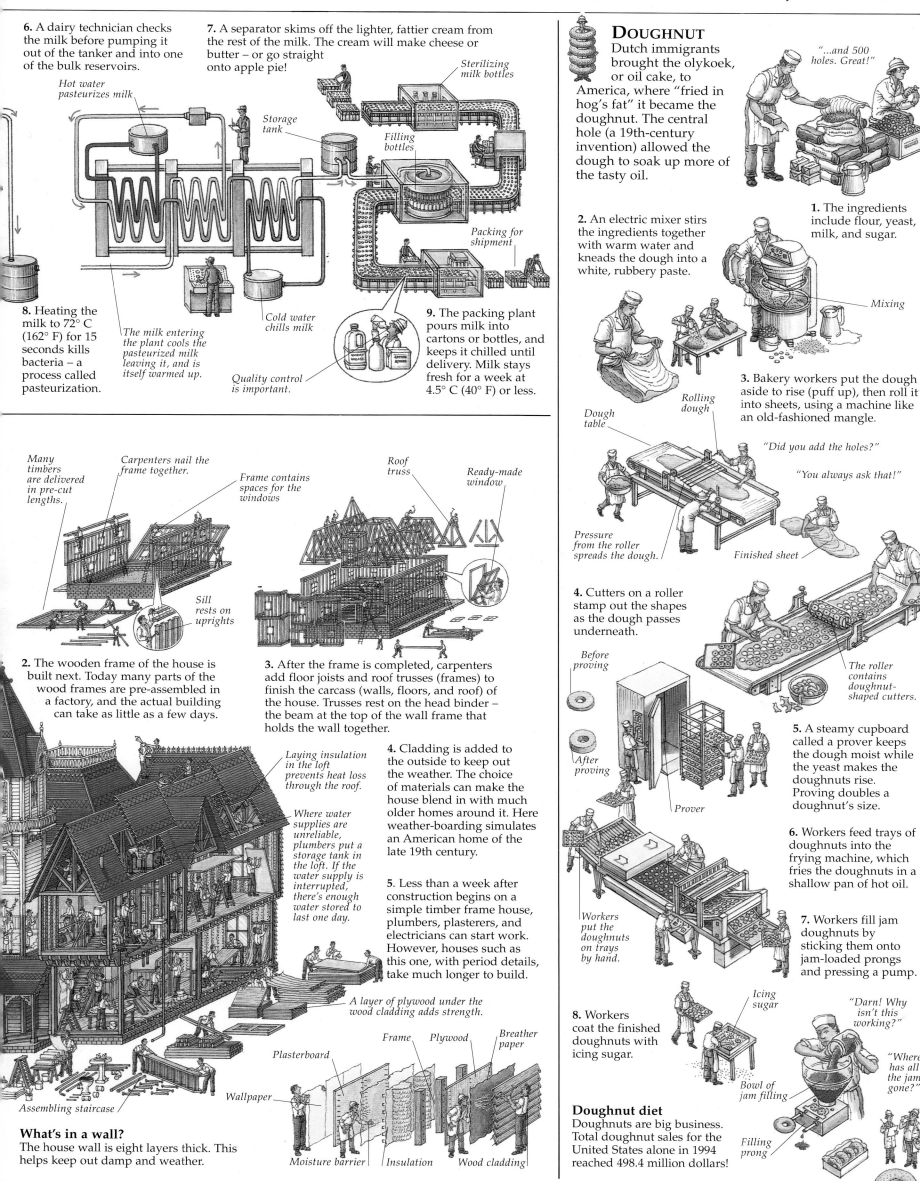

6. A dairy technician checks the milk before pumping it out of the tanker and into one of the bulk reservoirs.

7. A separator skims off the lighter, fattier cream from the rest of the milk. The cream will make cheese or butter – or go straight onto apple pie!

Hot water pasteurizes milk

Sterilizing milk bottles

Storage tank

Filling bottles

Packing for shipment

8. Heating the milk to 72° C (162° F) for 15 seconds kills bacteria – a process called pasteurization.

The milk entering the plant cools the pasteurized milk leaving it, and is itself warmed up.

Cold water chills milk

Quality control is important.

9. The packing plant pours milk into cartons or bottles, and keeps it chilled until delivery. Milk stays fresh for a week at 4.5° C (40° F) or less.

Many timbers are delivered in pre-cut lengths.

Carpenters nail the frame together.

Frame contains spaces for the windows

Roof truss

Ready-made window

Sill rests on uprights

2. The wooden frame of the house is built next. Today many parts of the wood frames are pre-assembled in a factory, and the actual building can take as little as a few days.

3. After the frame is completed, carpenters add floor joists and roof trusses (frames) to finish the carcass (walls, floors, and roof) of the house. Trusses rest on the head binder – the beam at the top of the wall frame that holds the wall together.

Laying insulation in the loft prevents heat loss through the roof.

Where water supplies are unreliable, plumbers put a storage tank in the loft. If the water supply is interrupted, there's enough water stored to last one day.

4. Cladding is added to the outside to keep out the weather. The choice of materials can make the house blend in with much older homes around it. Here weather-boarding simulates an American home of the late 19th century.

5. Less than a week after construction begins on a simple timber frame house, plumbers, plasterers, and electricians can start work. However, houses such as this one, with period details, take much longer to build.

A layer of plywood under the wood cladding adds strength.

Assembling staircase

What's in a wall?
The house wall is eight layers thick. This helps keep out damp and weather.

Wallpaper | *Plasterboard* | *Frame* | *Plywood* | *Breather paper*

Moisture barrier | *Insulation* | *Wood cladding*

DOUGHNUT
Dutch immigrants brought the olykoek, or oil cake, to America, where "fried in hog's fat" it became the doughnut. The central hole (a 19th-century invention) allowed the dough to soak up more of the tasty oil.

"...and 500 holes. Great!"

1. The ingredients include flour, yeast, milk, and sugar.

2. An electric mixer stirs the ingredients together with warm water and kneads the dough into a white, rubbery paste.

Mixing

3. Bakery workers put the dough aside to rise (puff up), then roll it into sheets, using a machine like an old-fashioned mangle.

Dough table

Rolling dough

"Did you add the holes?"

"You always ask that!"

Pressure from the roller spreads the dough.

Finished sheet

4. Cutters on a roller stamp out the shapes as the dough passes underneath.

The roller contains doughnut-shaped cutters.

Before proving

After proving

5. A steamy cupboard called a prover keeps the dough moist while the yeast makes the doughnuts rise. Proving doubles a doughnut's size.

Prover

6. Workers feed trays of doughnuts into the frying machine, which fries the doughnuts in a shallow pan of hot oil.

Workers put the doughnuts on trays by hand.

7. Workers fill jam doughnuts by sticking them onto jam-loaded prongs and pressing a pump.

Icing sugar

8. Workers coat the finished doughnuts with icing sugar.

"Darn! Why isn't this working?"

"Where has all the jam gone?"

Bowl of jam filling

Filling prong

Doughnut diet
Doughnuts are big business. Total doughnut sales for the United States alone in 1994 reached 498.4 million dollars!

COMPACT DISC

A compact disc can store up to 80 minutes of music, or more than 100 million words – the equivalent of almost 500 books.

Washing   *Coating*   *Oven drying*

Digitally recorded music is converted to a laser signal.

Production workers dress like surgeons to keep dust from marring the discs.

Developing

The metal layer is separated from the glass master.

Electroforming

"Father"   *"Mother"*   *"Son"*

Electroformed master   *"Mother"*

1. Washed glass discs are coated with a special solution and dried. This prepares the surface for the laser "cutting" machine.

2. Music recorded digitally (as on-off signals) controls a laser, which burns a series of tiny dots on the disc surface.

3. Developing fluid etches the burnt areas, forming pits. Electroforming follows. This deposits nickel on the glass master.

4. The metal layer ("father") has a negative impression. It is used to create several positives ("mothers").

STEAM LOCOMOTIVE

Locomotives powered by steam once hauled every train. Heat from a coal fire in the locomotive's firebox boiled water in the boiler to create steam. The pressurized steam then pushed on pistons contained within the locomotive's cylinders. This power drove the wheels via metal connecting rods. Some locomotives covered three times the distance to the moon and back in their working lives. Locomotive factories built them from scratch: raw materials went in one gate, and completed locomotives steamed out of another.

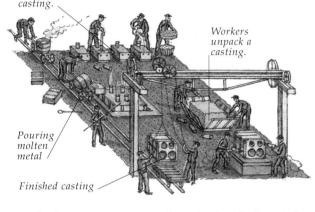

Foundry workers made by hand the moulds used for casting.

Workers unpack a casting.

Pouring molten metal

Finished casting

A narrow-gauge railway moved heavy objects within the works.

Steam hammer

The machined cylinder block moved to the next stage.

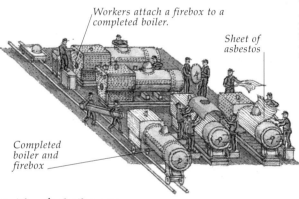

Workers attach a firebox to a completed boiler.

Sheet of asbestos

Completed boiler and firebox

5. After the boiler was assembled, it was attached to the firebox, where coal was burnt to turn water into steam. Then the boiler was insulated with sheets of asbestos (mineral fibre) to prevent heat loss.

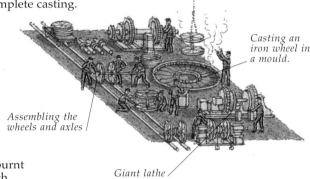

Casting an iron wheel in a mould.

Assembling the wheels and axles

Giant lathe

1. The first step was to cast the cylinder blocks. Workers packed sand around wooden patterns to create half-moulds. They then removed the patterns and united the halves. Pouring in hot iron created a complete casting.

2. In the metalworking shop, smiths machined the castings precisely and hammered other parts into shape using a huge steam-powered hammer. The sound of the steam hammer travelled a long way.

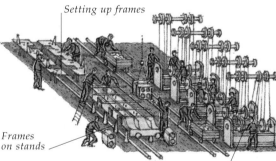

Setting up frames

Frames on stands

The lathes were belt-driven from a central source.

6. The locomotive rolled along on cast-iron wheels. These were cast next. Steel tyres were fitted onto the wheels to make a tough, wear-resistant rim. Boys as young as 13 shaped the wheels on giant lathes.

7. In the erecting shop, workers assembled the frames. Until the wheels were completed, the frames rested on cone-shaped stands. Other workers machined precision parts on lathes.

MATCHES

Friction matches were invented by British chemist John Walker in 1827. Before this date, tinder boxes were used to make fire. A spark was made by striking a flint, lighting the tinder in the box.

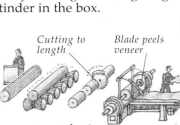

Cutting to length

Blade peels veneer

Sheet of veneer

Close-up of splints

1. Logs arrive at the factory and are cut to length. A machine then peels off veneer – thin sheets of wood.

2. Stacks of veneer are sliced into "splints" by a giant blade, making about two million every hour.

Fire retardant dip   *Drying splints*

Splints are fed into a blower to go to the match-making machine.

3. Sieving removes splints that are the wrong size. A dip in fire retardant liquid ensures that they don't smoulder after use.

4. The splints are dried, then tumbled in a drum to smooth them. They are then blown along tubes to the match-making machine.

5. The match-making machine is the size of two double-decker buses. An endless belt winds through it. The belt grips the matches at one end, and carries them through the machine.

Finished splints

A belt holds the matches in neat rows.

6. To make the match burn fiercely once it has ignited, each splint passes through a trough of paraffin wax. The path of the belt ensures that only the tips are coated.

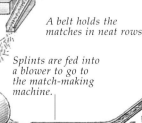
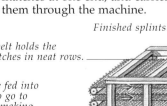

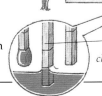

The match head is dipped in a chemical mixture.

The waxed area extends beyond the match head.

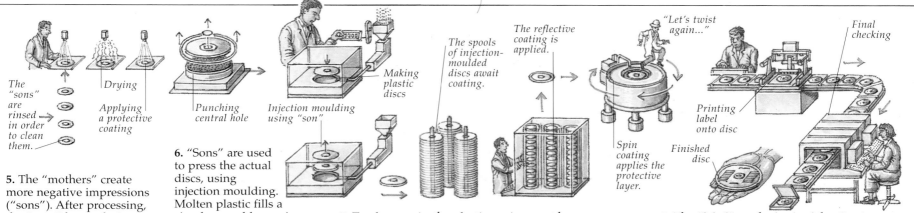

The "sons" are rinsed in order to clean them.

Drying

Applying a protective coating

Punching central hole

Injection moulding using "son"

Making plastic discs

The spools of injection-moulded discs await coating.

The reflective coating is applied.

"Let's twist again..."

Final checking

Printing label onto disc

Spin coating applies the protective layer.

Finished disc

5. The "mothers" create more negative impressions ("sons"). After processing, the "sons" have a hole stamped in the middle and their edges trimmed.

6. "Sons" are used to press the actual discs, using injection moulding. Molten plastic fills a circular mould, copying the pattern of pits from the "son".

7. To play music, the plastic copies must have a reflective metallic layer applied. A further transparent coating protects the delicate surface from damage.

8. The "label" on the back of the disc is printed on, and the discs undergo final checks before packing in plastic "jewel cases".

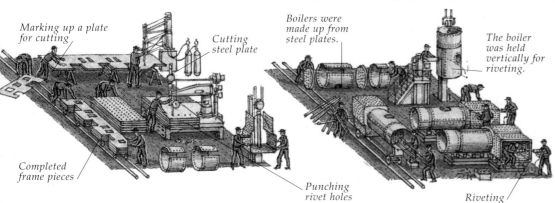

Marking up a plate for cutting

Cutting steel plate

Completed frame pieces

Boilers were made up from steel plates.

The boiler was held vertically for riveting.

Punching rivet holes

Riveting

3. In the frame shop, workers cut out the locomotive's frames from thick metal plates. The shapes were marked with chalk. After cutting, holes were drilled to take the rivets that held the locomotive together.

4. The next step was to make the boiler. Workers marked, cut, and drilled the boiler plates. Riveters hammered flat the hot rivet heads, joining the plates together. The noise made boilermakers deaf.

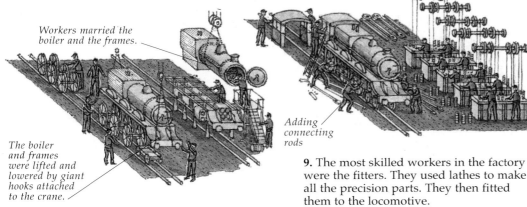

Workers married the boiler and the frames.

The boiler and frames were lifted and lowered by giant hooks attached to the crane.

Adding connecting rods

Workers painted the locomotive by hand.

8. Next, the boiler/firebox assembly was attached to the completed frames. Then a huge crane lifted the boiler and frames, and lowered them onto the assembled pairs of wheels.

9. The most skilled workers in the factory were the fitters. They used lathes to make all the precision parts. They then fitted them to the locomotive.

10. Finally, the locomotive got a coat of paint before being steamed up for a test run. At their peak around 1895, steam locomotive factories were vast, and employed entire towns.

7. A similar trough contains the chemical that forms the match head. For safety matches, the chemical will only catch fire when rubbed on the striking surface of the box.

8. Outer sections of the boxes are made separately, and move through on a conveyor ready to meet the filled trays.

9. Completed matches drop from the machine into prepared boxes. Another machine puts the inner and outer boxes together. The matches are then ready for quality testing, packing, and despatch.

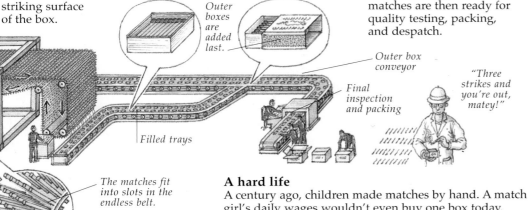

Outer boxes are added last.

Outer box conveyor

Final inspection and packing

"Three strikes and you're out, matey!"

Filled trays

The matches fit into slots in the endless belt.

A hard life
A century ago, children made matches by hand. A match girl's daily wages wouldn't even buy one box today.

DIAMOND RING

To find a perfect diamond big enough to cut into a one-carat (0.2 gram) gem, diamond miners may have to dig out enough rock to fill a medium-sized block of flats. Although diamonds are rare gemstones, advertising exaggerates their value; only larger, perfect stones are really precious.

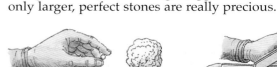

Split stone

A rough diamond is much bigger than the finished stone.

1. Rough (newly mined) diamonds look dull – a far cry from the finished stone.

2. Diamond cutters remove imperfections by cleaving the stone along its natural grain.

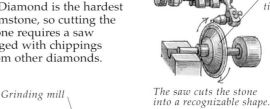

Diamond-tipped blade

3. Diamond is the hardest gemstone, so cutting the stone requires a saw edged with chippings from other diamonds.

The saw cuts the stone into a recognizable shape.

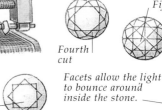

Grinding mill

First cut

Second cut

Third cut

Fourth cut

Fifth cut

Sixth cut

Facets allow the light to bounce around inside the stone.

4. Facets (flat faces) make diamonds twinkle. A special mill grinds the facets on the stone one by one.

5. The 58 facets of a "brilliant" diamond are made by repeatedly grinding and polishing the stone.

Gold strip

Mandrel

6. The jeweller forms a ring by hammering a gold strip and soldering it together.

7. Gently hammering the ring on a mandrel (a round anvil) shapes it into a precise circle.

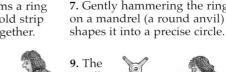

8. Filing and stretching adjusts the size, so that it fits the wearer's finger.

9. The jeweller makes the setting by cutting the shape and bending the prongs to grip the stone.

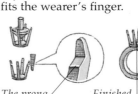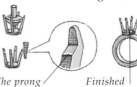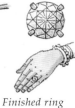

The prong holds the stone in place when bent over.

Finished setting

Mounting the diamond lets light in underneath so that the stone sparkles.

Finished ring

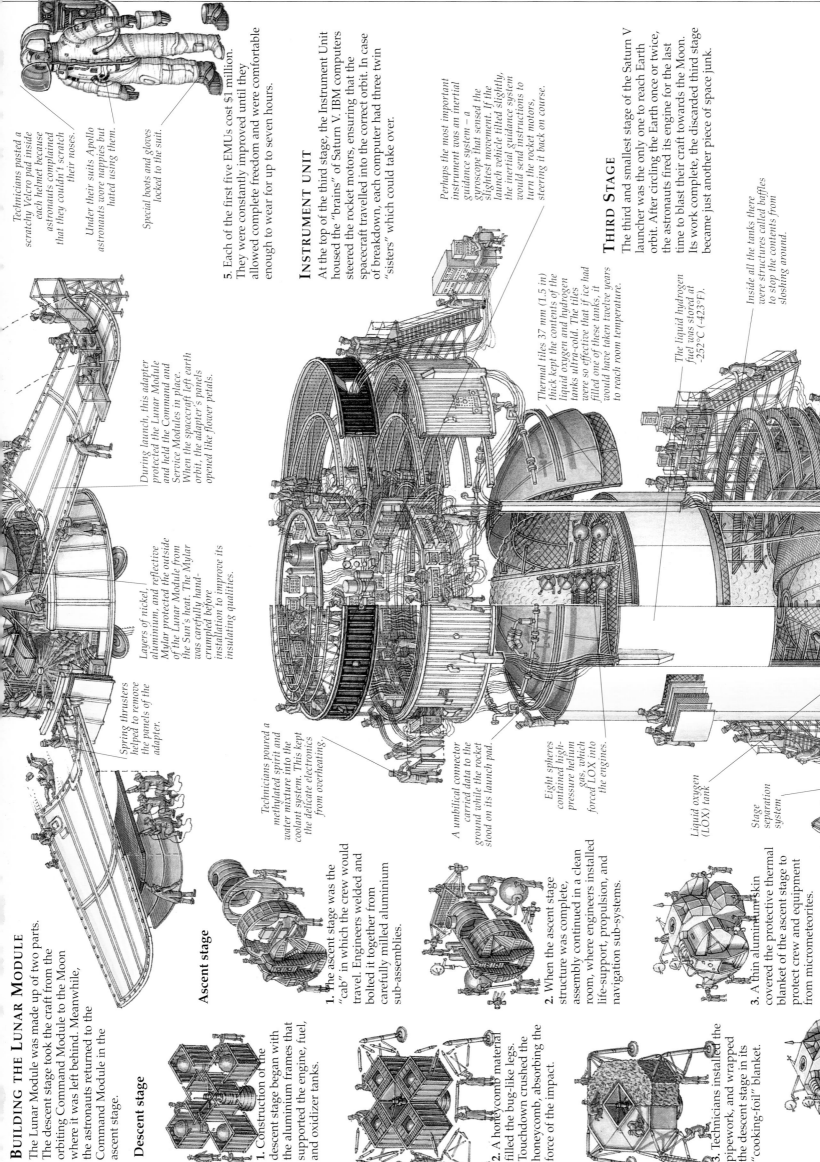

5. Each of the first five EMUs cost $1 million. They were constantly improved until they allowed complete freedom and were comfortable enough to wear for up to seven hours.

INSTRUMENT UNIT

At the top of the third stage, the Instrument Unit housed the "brains" of Saturn V. IBM computers steered the rocket motors, ensuring that the spacecraft travelled into the correct orbit. In case of breakdown, each computer had three twin "sisters" which could take over.

Perhaps the most important instrument was an inertial guidance system – a gyroscope that sensed the slightest movement. If the launch vehicle tilted slightly, the inertial guidance system would send instructions to turn the rocket motors, steering it back on course.

THIRD STAGE

The third and smallest stage of the Saturn V launcher was the only one to reach Earth orbit. After circling the Earth once or twice, the astronauts fired its engine for the last time to blast their craft towards the Moon. Its work complete, the discarded third stage became just another piece of space junk.

The third stage had just one J2 engine to provide power. Manufacturers Rocketdyne test-fired the J2 engine 2,500 times on the ground to check its reliability and to measure thrust.

A service tunnel carried power and control cables along the exterior. More than 2,500,000 soldered joints linked these cables.

Inside all the tanks there were structures called baffles to stop the contents from sloshing around.

The liquid hydrogen fuel was stored at -252°C (-423°F).

Thermal tiles 37 mm (1.5 in) thick kept the contents of the liquid oxygen and hydrogen tanks ultra-cold. The tiles were so effective that if ice had filled one of these tanks, it would have taken twelve years to reach room room temperature.

Liquid oxygen (LOX) tank

Stage separation system

Eight spheres contained high-pressure helium gas, which forced LOX into the engines.

A umbilical connector carried data to the rocket while the rocket stood on its launch pad.

Technicians poured a methylated spirit and water mixture into the coolant system. This kept the delicate electronics from overheating.

BUILDING THE LUNAR MODULE

The Lunar Module was made up of two parts. The descent stage took the craft from the orbiting Command Module to the Moon where it was left behind. Meanwhile, the astronauts returned to the Command Module in the ascent stage.

Descent stage

1. Construction of the descent stage began with the aluminium frames that supported the engine, fuel, and oxidizer tanks.

Ascent stage

1. The ascent stage was the "cab" in which the crew would travel. Engineers welded and bolted it together from carefully milled aluminium sub-assemblies.

2. When the ascent stage structure was complete, assembly continued in a clean room, where engineers installed life-support, propulsion, and navigation sub-systems.

2. A honeycomb material filled the bug-like legs. Touchdown crushed the honeycomb, absorbing the force of the impact.

3. Technicians installed the pipework, and wrapped the descent stage in its "cooking-foil" blanket.

3. A thin aluminium skin covered the protective thermal blanket of the ascent stage to protect crew and equipment from micrometeorites.

Assembly

When each stage was complete, the two were finally put together.

During launch, this adapter protected the Lunar Module and held the Command and Service Modules in place. When the spacecraft left earth orbit, the adapter's panels opened like flower petals.

Layers of nickel, aluminium, and reflective Mylar protected the outside of the Lunar Module from the Sun's heat. The Mylar was carefully hand-crumpled before installation to improve its insulating qualities.

Spring thrusters helped to remove the panels of the adapter.

SATURN V

WHEN THE AMERICAN SPACE PROGRAMME FINALLY
achieved a Moon landing on 20 July 1969, the
Apollo 11 spacecraft was launched by a
powerful rocket called Saturn V. The most
powerful rocket ever, Saturn V was
used to launch all the Apollo spacecraft on lunar missions.
The rocket alone stood 110 metres (363 feet) high and
had three stages, each of which fell away when it ran out
of fuel. To follow what happened as Saturn V took off,
start at the first stage at the bottom right of the page.

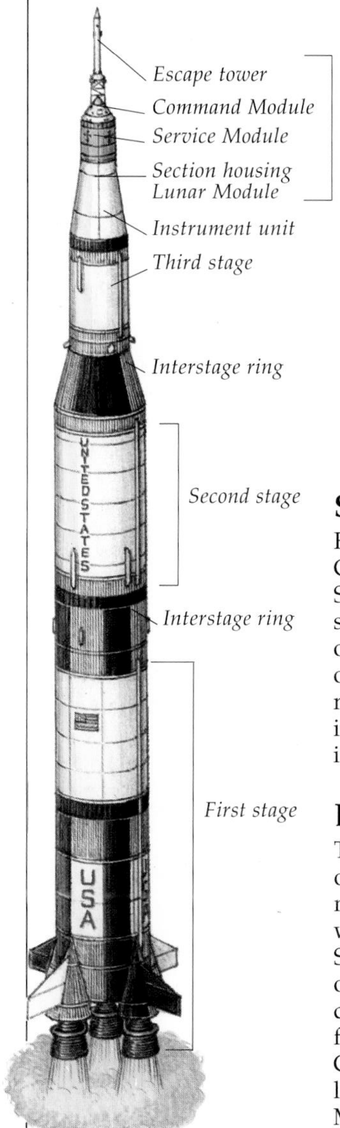

LIFT-OFF!
The picture above shows how
the three stages of the rocket
and the sections of the
spacecraft fitted together.

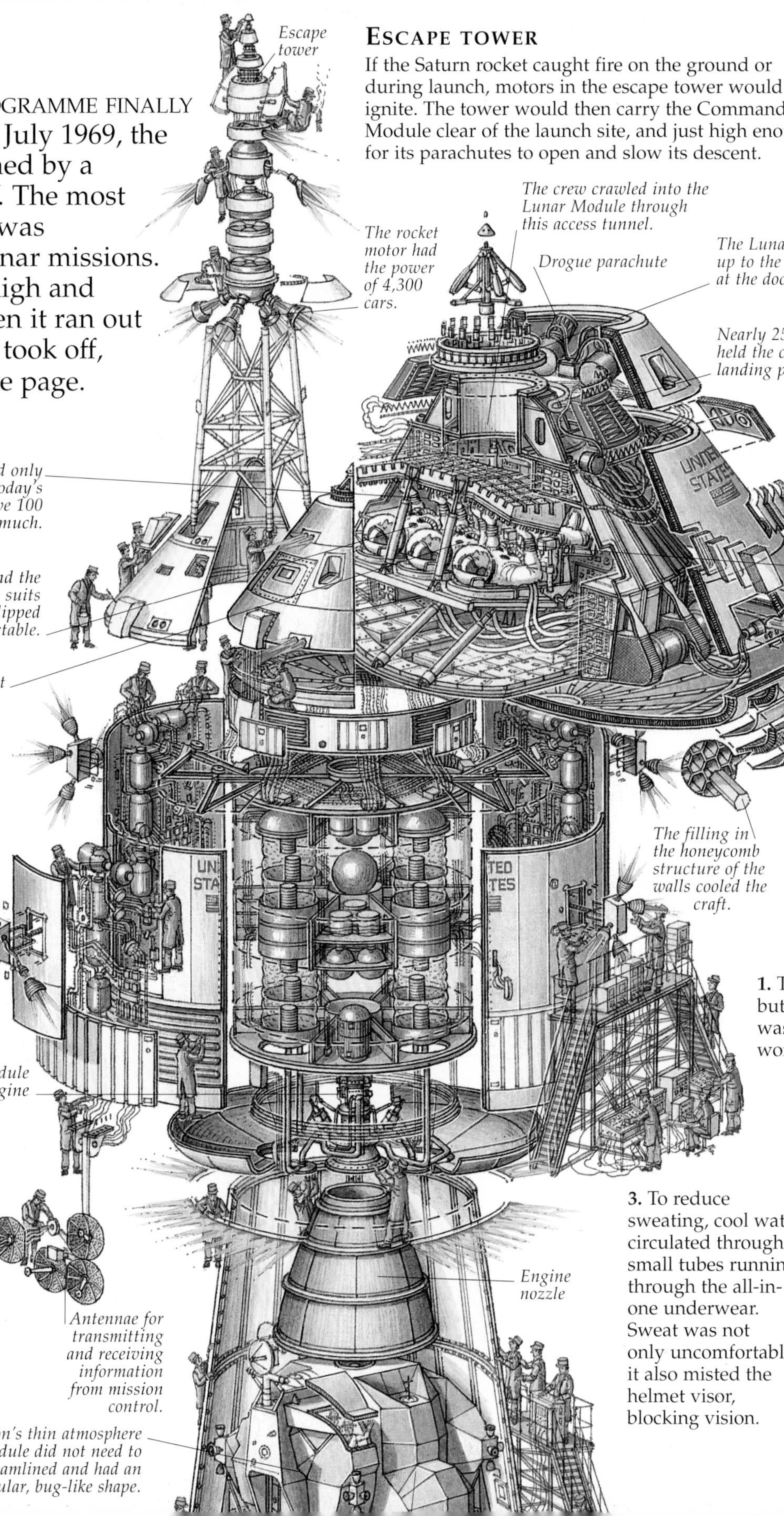

*Apollo
spacecraft*

- Escape tower
- Command Module
- Service Module
- Section housing
  Lunar Module
- Instrument unit
- Third stage

- Interstage ring
- Second stage

- Interstage ring
- First stage

SERVICE MODULE

Fixed to the base of the
Command Module, the tubular
Service Module carried
supplies of fuel and
oxidizer, plus water and
oxygen for the crew. Its rocket
motor moved the spacecraft
into Moon orbit, and powered
it back to Earth.

*The Mission Commander and the
other astronauts wore their suits
during the launch, but later slipped
into something more comfortable.*

*The flight computer had only
32k of memory – today's
home computers have 100
times as much.*

*Small jets were positioned all
around the spacecraft.
Controlling the firing of these
rockets enabled the astronauts
to turn the craft.*

Command Module pilot

*Service Module
engine*

LUNAR MODULE

The Lunar Module was the only part
of the Apollo 11 mission to land on the
moon. On launch, the Lunar Module
was fixed below the Command and
Service Modules (CSM). Once
out of Earth orbit, the petal-like
doors protecting the Lunar Module
fell away. The crew then separated the
CSM, turned it upside down and
linked up with the exposed Lunar
Module. Finally, springs separated the
Lunar Module from the third stage.

*In the Moon's thin atmosphere
the Lunar Module did not need to
be streamlined and had an
angular, bug-like shape.*

*Antennae for
transmitting
and receiving
information
from mission
control.*

*Engine
nozzle*

ESCAPE TOWER

If the Saturn rocket caught fire on the ground or
during launch, motors in the escape tower would
ignite. The tower would then carry the Command
Module clear of the launch site, and just high enough
for its parachutes to open and slow its descent.

*Escape
tower*

*The rocket
motor had
the power
of 4,300
cars.*

*The crew crawled into the
Lunar Module through
this access tunnel.*

Drogue parachute

*The Lunar Module linked
up to the Command Module
at the docking ring.*

*Nearly 250 nylon strands
held the capsule to the
landing parachutes.*

*The heat shield
was made up of
seven different
layers.*

*Lunar
Module
pilot*

COMMAND MODULE

During their journey to the Moon, the astronauts lived
in the Command Module. While two of them
descended to the lunar surface, the third stayed behind
in the orbiting craft. Building this capsule was perhaps
the most complex task of the Apollo programme: it
had over two million parts (a car has around 2,000).

1. The pressurized crew compartment
was only a little larger than a compact
car, but in this small space the astronauts
had to eat, sleep, work, and keep clean
for over a week.

2. Special shields surrounded the
Command Module to protect it from the
intense heat generated by re-entering the
Earth's atmosphere. The Command
Module fell through the atmosphere
until it was 7,300 m (24,000 feet) above
the ocean. Then small "drogue"
parachutes opened to slow the descent.
The main parachutes opened later,
slowing the craft enough to splash into
the ocean safely.

SPACE SUIT

On the Moon, Extravehicular Mobility Units
(EMUs or space suits) protected astronauts from
the vacuum of space, and from heat, cold,
radiation, and meteors. Each astronaut had three
tailor-made EMUs: one mission suit, one
training suit, and one backup suit.

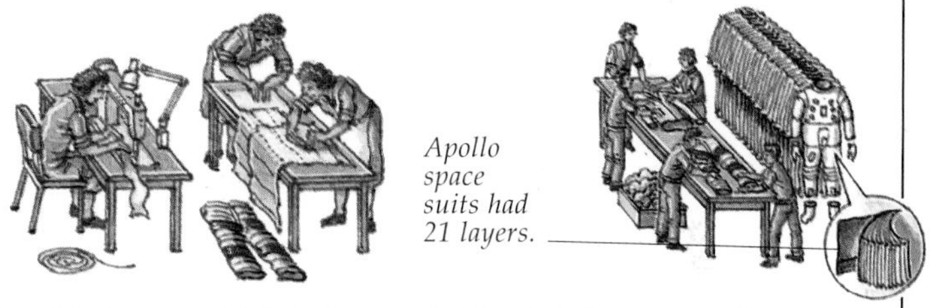

*Apollo
space
suits had
21 layers.*

1. The fabrics were high-tech
but the construction process
was conventional and expert
workers sewed the seams.

*The filling in
the honeycomb
structure of the
walls cooled the
craft.*

2. The EMU was actually
three garments: liquid-cooled
underwear, a pressurized
suit, and a protective cover.

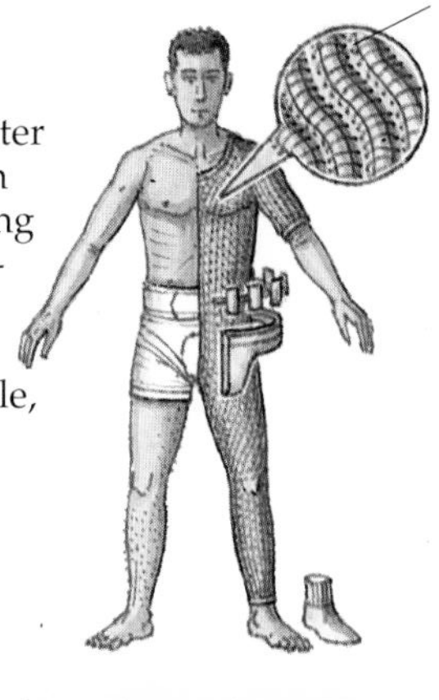

*Small tubes
were sewn into
the fabric of the
underwear.*

3. To reduce
sweating, cool water
circulated through
small tubes running
through the all-in-
one underwear.
Sweat was not
only uncomfortable,
it also misted the
helmet visor,
blocking vision.

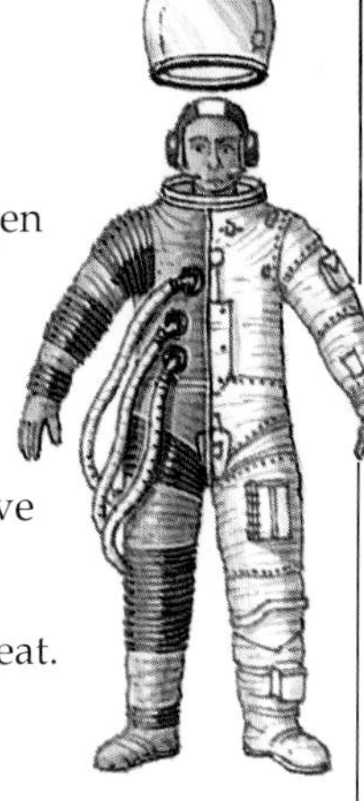

4. Hoses at chest
level carried oxygen
from the suit
through the
Portable Life
Support System
(PLSS), which
filtered it to remove
carbon dioxide,
flatulence, and
moisture from sweat.

BRIDGE

HOW CAN A STEEL WIRE THE THICKNESS OF a pencil hold up the longest bridge in the world? The massive span does not snap the thin wire because it is bound into thick cables. The cables can support the weight of huge lorries, and withstand violent winds.

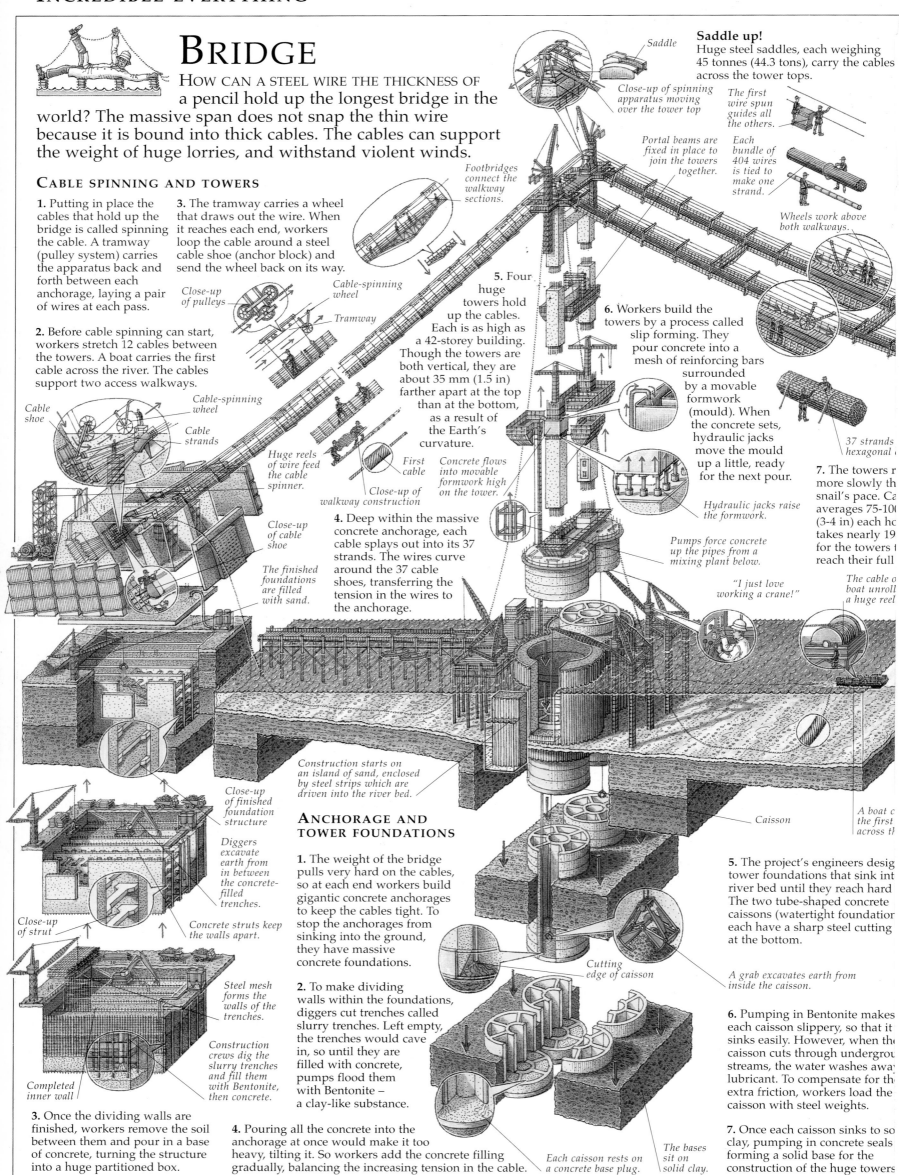

CABLE SPINNING AND TOWERS

1. Putting in place the cables that hold up the bridge is called spinning the cable. A tramway (pulley system) carries the apparatus back and forth between each anchorage, laying a pair of wires at each pass.

2. Before cable spinning can start, workers stretch 12 cables between the towers. A boat carries the first cable across the river. The cables support two access walkways.

3. The tramway carries a wheel that draws out the wire. When it reaches each end, workers loop the cable around a steel cable shoe (anchor block) and send the wheel back on its way.

4. Deep within the massive concrete anchorage, each cable splays out into its 37 strands. The wires curve around the 37 cable shoes, transferring the tension in the wires to the anchorage.

5. Four huge towers hold up the cables. Each is as high as a 42-storey building. Though the towers are both vertical, they are about 35 mm (1.5 in) farther apart at the top than at the bottom, as a result of the Earth's curvature.

6. Workers build the towers by a process called slip forming. They pour concrete into a mesh of reinforcing bars surrounded by a movable formwork (mould). When the concrete sets, hydraulic jacks move the mould up a little, ready for the next pour.

7. The towers r more slowly th snail's pace. Ca averages 75-10((3-4 in) each ho takes nearly 19 for the towers t reach their full

Labels (left side)
- Cable shoe
- Close-up of pulleys
- Cable-spinning wheel
- Tramway
- Cable-spinning wheel
- Cable strands
- Huge reels of wire feed the cable spinner.
- Close-up of cable shoe
- The finished foundations are filled with sand.
- First cable
- Close-up of walkway construction
- Concrete flows into movable formwork high on the tower.

Labels (right side)
- Saddle
- **Saddle up!** Huge steel saddles, each weighing 45 tonnes (44.3 tons), carry the cables across the tower tops.
- Close-up of spinning apparatus moving over the tower top
- The first wire spun guides all the others.
- Portal beams are fixed in place to join the towers together.
- Each bundle of 404 wires is tied to make one strand.
- Wheels work above both walkways.
- Footbridges connect the walkway sections.
- 37 strands hexagonal
- Hydraulic jacks raise the formwork.
- Pumps force concrete up the pipes from a mixing plant below.
- "I just love working a crane!"
- The cable o boat unroll a huge reel

ANCHORAGE AND TOWER FOUNDATIONS

1. The weight of the bridge pulls very hard on the cables, so at each end workers build gigantic concrete anchorages to keep the cables tight. To stop the anchorages from sinking into the ground, they have massive concrete foundations.

2. To make dividing walls within the foundations, diggers cut trenches called slurry trenches. Left empty, the trenches would cave in, so until they are filled with concrete, pumps flood them with Bentonite – a clay-like substance.

3. Once the dividing walls are finished, workers remove the soil between them and pour in a base of concrete, turning the structure into a huge partitioned box.

4. Pouring all the concrete into the anchorage at once would make it too heavy, tilting it. So workers add the concrete filling gradually, balancing the increasing tension in the cable.

5. The project's engineers desig tower foundations that sink int river bed until they reach hard The two tube-shaped concrete caissons (watertight foundatior each have a sharp steel cutting at the bottom.

6. Pumping in Bentonite makes each caisson slippery, so that it sinks easily. However, when the caisson cuts through undergrou streams, the water washes awa lubricant. To compensate for th extra friction, workers load the caisson with steel weights.

7. Once each caisson sinks to so clay, pumping in concrete seals forming a solid base for the construction of the huge towers

Labels (lower)
- Close-up of finished foundation structure
- Diggers excavate earth from in between the concrete-filled trenches.
- Concrete struts keep the walls apart.
- Close-up of strut
- Steel mesh forms the walls of the trenches.
- Construction crews dig the slurry trenches and fill them with Bentonite, then concrete.
- Completed inner wall
- Construction starts on an island of sand, enclosed by steel strips which are driven into the river bed.
- Caisson
- A boat c the first across th
- Cutting edge of caisson
- A grab excavates earth from inside the caisson.
- Each caisson rests on a concrete base plug.
- The bases sit on solid clay.

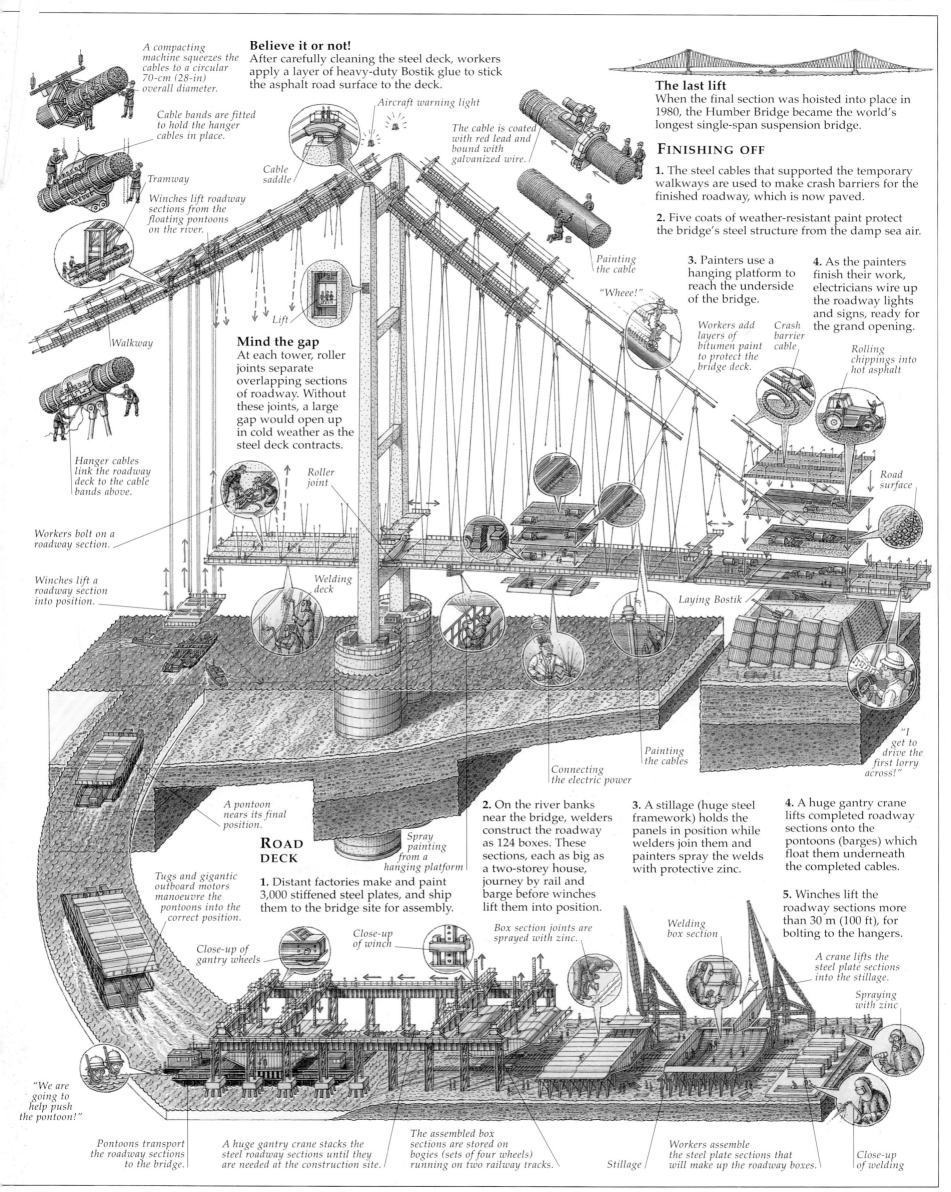

A compacting machine squeezes the cables to a circular 70-cm (28-in) overall diameter.

Cable bands are fitted to hold the hanger cables in place.

Tramway

Winches lift roadway sections from the floating pontoons on the river.

Walkway

Hanger cables link the roadway deck to the cable bands above.

Workers bolt on a roadway section.

Winches lift a roadway section into position.

Believe it or not!
After carefully cleaning the steel deck, workers apply a layer of heavy-duty Bostik glue to stick the asphalt road surface to the deck.

Aircraft warning light

Cable saddle

The cable is coated with red lead and bound with galvanized wire.

Lift

Mind the gap
At each tower, roller joints separate overlapping sections of roadway. Without these joints, a large gap would open up in cold weather as the steel deck contracts.

Roller joint

Welding deck

Painting the cable

The last lift
When the final section was hoisted into place in 1980, the Humber Bridge became the world's longest single-span suspension bridge.

FINISHING OFF

1. The steel cables that supported the temporary walkways are used to make crash barriers for the finished roadway, which is now paved.

2. Five coats of weather-resistant paint protect the bridge's steel structure from the damp sea air.

3. Painters use a hanging platform to reach the underside of the bridge.

4. As the painters finish their work, electricians wire up the roadway lights and signs, ready for the grand opening.

"Wheee!"

Workers add layers of bitumen paint to protect the bridge deck.

Crash barrier cable

Rolling chippings into hot asphalt

Road surface

Laying Bostik

Painting the cables

Connecting the electric power

"I get to drive the first lorry across!"

A pontoon nears its final position.

ROAD DECK

Tugs and gigantic outboard motors manoeuvre the pontoons into the correct position.

Spray painting from a hanging platform

1. Distant factories make and paint 3,000 stiffened steel plates, and ship them to the bridge site for assembly.

2. On the river banks near the bridge, welders construct the roadway as 124 boxes. These sections, each as big as a two-storey house, journey by rail and barge before winches lift them into position.

3. A stillage (huge steel framework) holds the panels in position while welders join them and painters spray the welds with protective zinc.

4. A huge gantry crane lifts completed roadway sections onto the pontoons (barges) which float them underneath the completed cables.

5. Winches lift the roadway sections more than 30 m (100 ft), for bolting to the hangers.

Welding box section

A crane lifts the steel plate sections into the stillage.

Spraying with zinc

"We are going to help push the pontoon!"

Close-up of gantry wheels

Close-up of winch

Box section joints are sprayed with zinc.

Pontoons transport the roadway sections to the bridge.

A huge gantry crane stacks the steel roadway sections until they are needed at the construction site.

The assembled box sections are stored on bogies (sets of four wheels) running on two railway tracks.

Stillage

Workers assemble the steel plate sections that will make up the roadway boxes.

Close-up of welding

INCREDIBLE EVERYTHING

CAR

Most modern car factories use robots for routine tasks such as welding and painting. Humans keep production flowing smoothly and monitor quality.

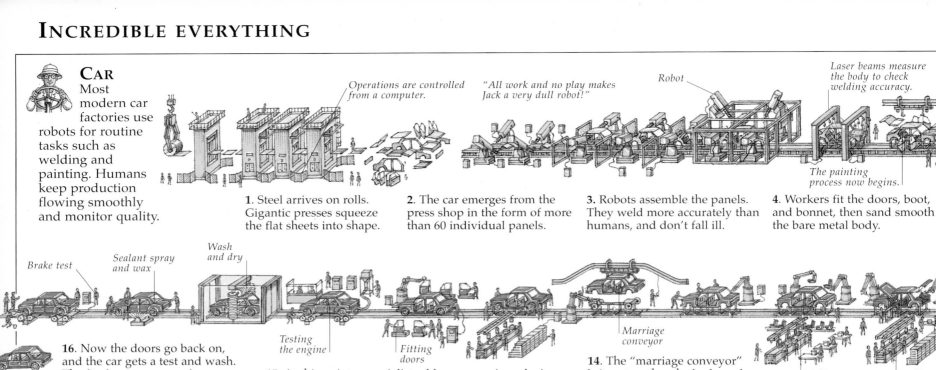

Operations are controlled from a computer.

"All work and no play makes Jack a very dull robot!"

Robot

Laser beams measure the body to check welding accuracy.

The painting process now begins.

1. Steel arrives on rolls. Gigantic presses squeeze the flat sheets into shape.

2. The car emerges from the press shop in the form of more than 60 individual panels.

3. Robots assemble the panels. They weld more accurately than humans, and don't fall ill.

4. Workers fit the doors, boot, and bonnet, then sand smooth the bare metal body.

Brake test

Sealant spray and wax

Wash and dry

Testing the engine

Fitting doors

Marriage conveyor

Making seats

Making dashboards

16. Now the doors go back on, and the car gets a test and wash. The final steps are a sealant spray, a wax, and a brake test.

15. At this point a specialist adds an annoying, elusive rattle, and installs the famous "new car" smell.

14. The "marriage conveyor" brings together the body and the engine components.

COIN

Making metal coins is an ancient craft, and can often be dangerous. In the 16th century, coin makers at London's Mint (coin factory) were made unwell by fumes from the melting metal. To guard their health, they drank from the skulls of executed criminals, which they believed would protect them.

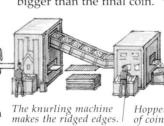

"What a relief!"

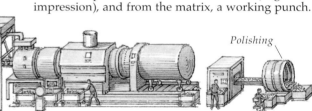

Plaster relief

Copy in metal

Reducing machine

Steel master punch

Copper ingot

Nickel is supplied in the form of pellets.

1. Copper is the main raw material for coins, although zinc and tin can also be used. Nickel is added to make the coins harder.

2. A coin starts life in a designer's studio. Then an artist uses plaster to model it as a relief (shallow sculpture).

3. From the relief, mint workers make an electrotype – a stronger copy in metal. This is bigger than the final coin.

4. A reducing machine cuts an exact replica, at a much smaller size, onto a steel master punch. From the master punch workers make a matrix (negative impression), and from the matrix, a working punch.

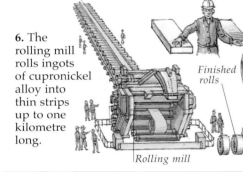

6. The rolling mill rolls ingots of cupronickel alloy into thin strips up to one kilometre long.

Finished rolls

Rolling mill

7. A blanking machine stamps out the basic round coin shape from the roll of alloy.

The knurling machine makes the ridged edges.

Hopper full of coin blanks

Polishing

8. A furnace anneals (heats) coins to soften them for stamping.

9. After processing, the coin blanks are dull. A polish brightens them up again.

ARMOUR

Well-made armour fitted like a good suit, and even fat knights could easily mount a horse. The invention of guns made armour obsolete – making the metal thick enough to stop bullets made armour too heavy to wear.

Clients chose their armour from a pattern book.

Marking metal

Shears were anchored in a tree trunk.

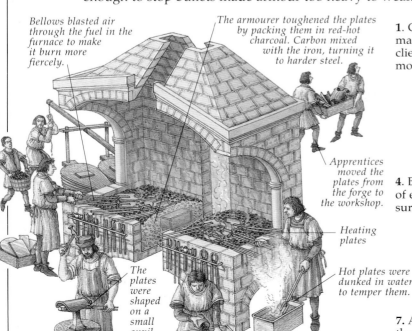

Bellows blasted air through the fuel in the furnace to make it burn more fiercely.

The armourer toughened the plates by packing them in red-hot charcoal. Carbon mixed with the iron, turning it to harder steel.

Apprentices moved the plates from the forge to the workshop.

Heating plates

The plates were shaped on a small anvil.

Hot plates were dunked in water to temper them.

1. Good quality armour was made to measure. Mail-order clients sent the armourer wax models of their limbs.

2. The armourer marked metal sheets with the outline of the different parts of the suit.

3. Next, the armourer or an apprentice cut out the basic shapes with large shears.

Polishing wheel

"Let me out of here!"

4. By carefully filing the edges of each plate, workers made sure that the suit fitted exactly.

5. Polishing was slow. To speed the process, armourers used large polishing wheels.

6. Decoration of armour made it more expensive. The best suits were etched with elaborate patterns.

"I hope it's strong enough!"

Making a suit of armour took about six weeks.

7. A locksmith made and fitted the fiddly bits, such as the hinges, buckles, and clasps.

8. Armourers tested their product by firing a crossbow at it. The dent this left demonstrated the armour's strength.

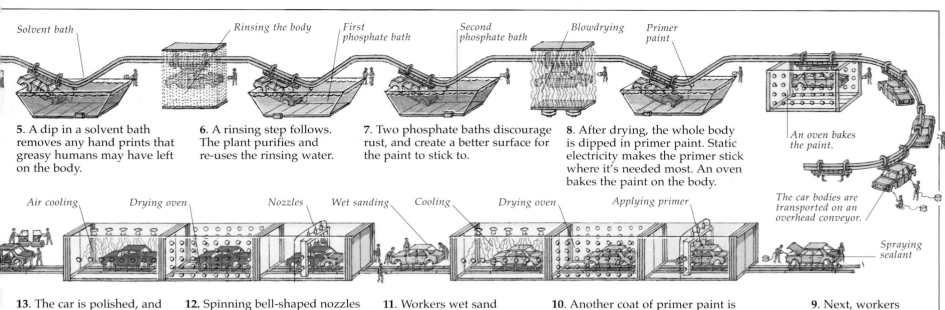

Solvent bath — *Rinsing the body* — *First phosphate bath* — *Second phosphate bath* — *Blowdrying* — *Primer paint*

An oven bakes the paint.

5. A dip in a solvent bath removes any hand prints that greasy humans may have left on the body.

6. A rinsing step follows. The plant purifies and re-uses the rinsing water.

7. Two phosphate baths discourage rust, and create a better surface for the paint to stick to.

8. After drying, the whole body is dipped in primer paint. Static electricity makes the primer stick where it's needed most. An oven bakes the paint on the body.

The car bodies are transported on an overhead conveyor.

Air cooling — *Drying oven* — *Nozzles* — *Wet sanding* — *Cooling* — *Drying oven* — *Applying primer*

Spraying sealant

13. The car is polished, and workers take off the doors, so the dashboard and seats can be installed.

12. Spinning bell-shaped nozzles spray on the coloured paint layer, and an oven bakes the paint hard. Then jets of air cool the body.

11. Workers wet sand the body to provide a firm surface for the next coat of paint.

10. Another coat of primer paint is applied. From this point on, all operations take place in filtered air, because specks of dust would spoil the car's shiny finish.

9. Next, workers spray sealant over areas of the car that might rust easily.

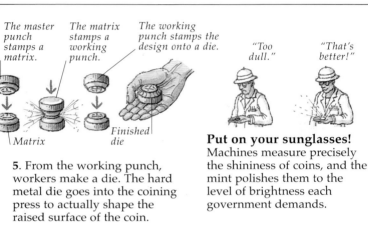

The master punch stamps a matrix.

The matrix stamps a working punch.

The working punch stamps the design onto a die.

"Too dull." — *"That's better!"*

Matrix — *Finished die*

5. From the working punch, workers make a die. The hard metal die goes into the coining press to actually shape the raised surface of the coin.

Put on your sunglasses! Machines measure precisely the shininess of coins, and the mint polishes them to the level of brightness each government demands.

Stamping the design completes the process.

Press stamps coin

Finished coin

10. The faces of the coin are stamped by the press. Then they are checked, weighed, and packed.

Indispensable discs Coins are expensive to make, but we use them for nearly two-thirds of our purchases.

PLASTIC BOTTLE

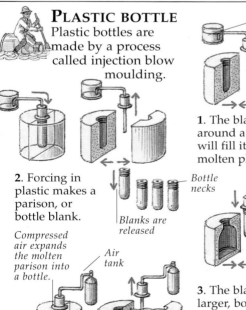

Plastic bottles are made by a process called injection blow moulding.

Molten plastic

2. Forcing in plastic makes a parison, or bottle blank.

Bottle necks

Blanks are released

Compressed air expands the molten parison into a bottle.

Air tank

1. The blank mould closes around a tube that will fill it with molten plastic.

3. The blank is moved to a larger, bottle-shaped mould, ready for heating and blowing.

The finished bottles are ready for filling.

Water cools mould

4. Forcing air into the heated blank inflates it to fill the mould.

5. After cooling, the mould opens and the bottle drops out.

DRINKING WATER

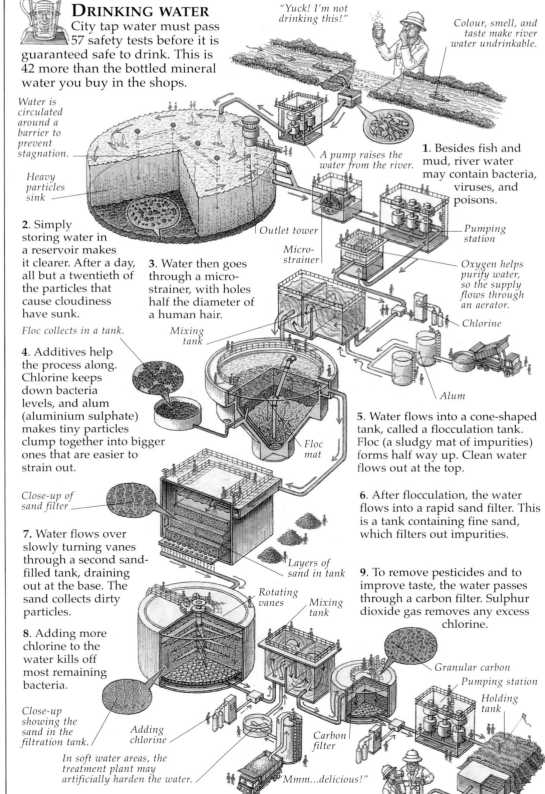

City tap water must pass 57 safety tests before it is guaranteed safe to drink. This is 42 more than the bottled mineral water you buy in the shops.

"Yuck! I'm not drinking this!"

Colour, smell, and taste make river water undrinkable.

Water is circulated around a barrier to prevent stagnation.

Heavy particles sink

A pump raises the water from the river.

1. Besides fish and mud, river water may contain bacteria, viruses, and poisons.

Outlet tower

Pumping station

2. Simply storing water in a reservoir makes it clearer. After a day, all but a twentieth of the particles that cause cloudiness have sunk.

Micro-strainer

3. Water then goes through a micro-strainer, with holes half the diameter of a human hair.

Oxygen helps purify water, so the supply flows through an aerator.

Floc collects in a tank.

Mixing tank

Chlorine

4. Additives help the process along. Chlorine keeps down bacteria levels, and alum (aluminium sulphate) makes tiny particles clump together into bigger ones that are easier to strain out.

Alum

5. Water flows into a cone-shaped tank, called a flocculation tank. Floc (a sludgy mat of impurities) forms half way up. Clean water flows out at the top.

Close-up of sand filter

Floc mat

6. After flocculation, the water flows into a rapid sand filter. This is a tank containing fine sand, which filters out impurities.

7. Water flows over slowly turning vanes through a second sand-filled tank, draining out at the base. The sand collects dirty particles.

Layers of sand in tank

Rotating vanes

Mixing tank

9. To remove pesticides and to improve taste, the water passes through a carbon filter. Sulphur dioxide gas removes any excess chlorine.

8. Adding more chlorine to the water kills off most remaining bacteria.

Granular carbon

Pumping station

Close-up showing the sand in the filtration tank.

Adding chlorine

Carbon filter

Holding tank

In soft water areas, the treatment plant may artificially harden the water.

"Mmm...delicious!"

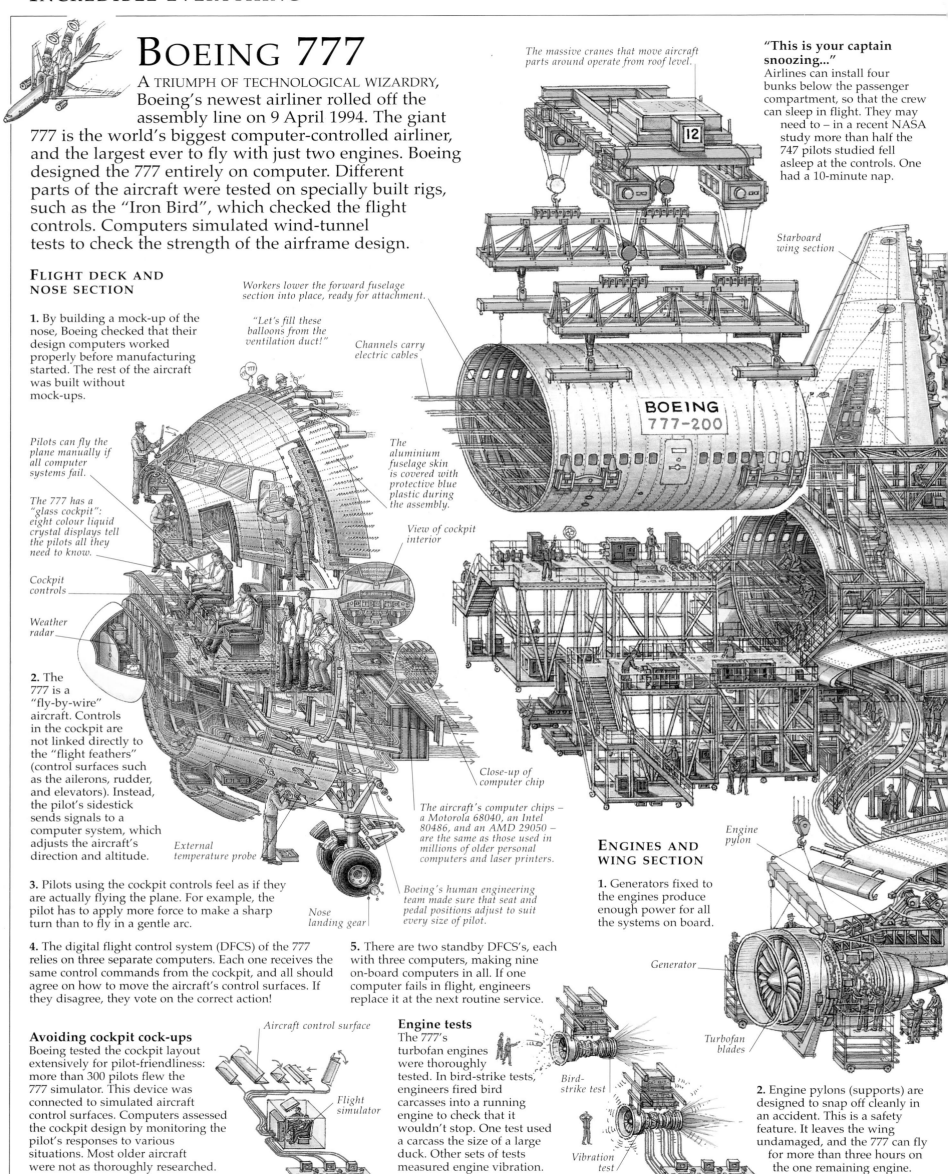

BOEING 777

A TRIUMPH OF TECHNOLOGICAL WIZARDRY, Boeing's newest airliner rolled off the assembly line on 9 April 1994. The giant 777 is the world's biggest computer-controlled airliner, and the largest ever to fly with just two engines. Boeing designed the 777 entirely on computer. Different parts of the aircraft were tested on specially built rigs, such as the "Iron Bird", which checked the flight controls. Computers simulated wind-tunnel tests to check the strength of the airframe design.

FLIGHT DECK AND NOSE SECTION

1. By building a mock-up of the nose, Boeing checked that their design computers worked properly before manufacturing started. The rest of the aircraft was built without mock-ups.

Pilots can fly the plane manually if all computer systems fail.

The 777 has a "glass cockpit": eight colour liquid crystal displays tell the pilots all they need to know.

Cockpit controls

Weather radar

2. The 777 is a "fly-by-wire" aircraft. Controls in the cockpit are not linked directly to the "flight feathers" (control surfaces such as the ailerons, rudder, and elevators). Instead, the pilot's sidestick sends signals to a computer system, which adjusts the aircraft's direction and altitude.

External temperature probe

Nose landing gear

3. Pilots using the cockpit controls feel as if they are actually flying the plane. For example, the pilot has to apply more force to make a sharp turn than to fly in a gentle arc.

4. The digital flight control system (DFCS) of the 777 relies on three separate computers. Each one receives the same control commands from the cockpit, and all should agree on how to move the aircraft's control surfaces. If they disagree, they vote on the correct action!

5. There are two standby DFCS's, each with three computers, making nine on-board computers in all. If one computer fails in flight, engineers replace it at the next routine service.

Avoiding cockpit cock-ups

Boeing tested the cockpit layout extensively for pilot-friendliness: more than 300 pilots flew the 777 simulator. This device was connected to simulated aircraft control surfaces. Computers assessed the cockpit design by monitoring the pilot's responses to various situations. Most older aircraft were not as thoroughly researched.

Aircraft control surface

Flight simulator

The massive cranes that move aircraft parts around operate from roof level.

Workers lower the forward fuselage section into place, ready for attachment.

"Let's fill these balloons from the ventilation duct!"

Channels carry electric cables

The aluminium fuselage skin is covered with protective blue plastic during the assembly.

BOEING 777-200

View of cockpit interior

Close-up of computer chip

The aircraft's computer chips – a Motorola 68040, an Intel 80486, and an AMD 29050 – are the same as those used in millions of older personal computers and laser printers.

Boeing's human engineering team made sure that seat and pedal positions adjust to suit every size of pilot.

Engine tests

The 777's turbofan engines were thoroughly tested. In bird-strike tests, engineers fired bird carcasses into a running engine to check that it wouldn't stop. One test used a carcass the size of a large duck. Other sets of tests measured engine vibration.

Bird-strike test

Vibration test

Starboard wing section

ENGINES AND WING SECTION

1. Generators fixed to the engines produce enough power for all the systems on board.

Engine pylon

Generator

Turbofan blades

2. Engine pylons (supports) are designed to snap off cleanly in an accident. This is a safety feature. It leaves the wing undamaged, and the 777 can fly for more than three hours on the one remaining engine.

"This is your captain snoozing..."

Airlines can install four bunks below the passenger compartment, so that the crew can sleep in flight. They may need to – in a recent NASA study more than half the 747 pilots studied fell asleep at the controls. One had a 10-minute nap.

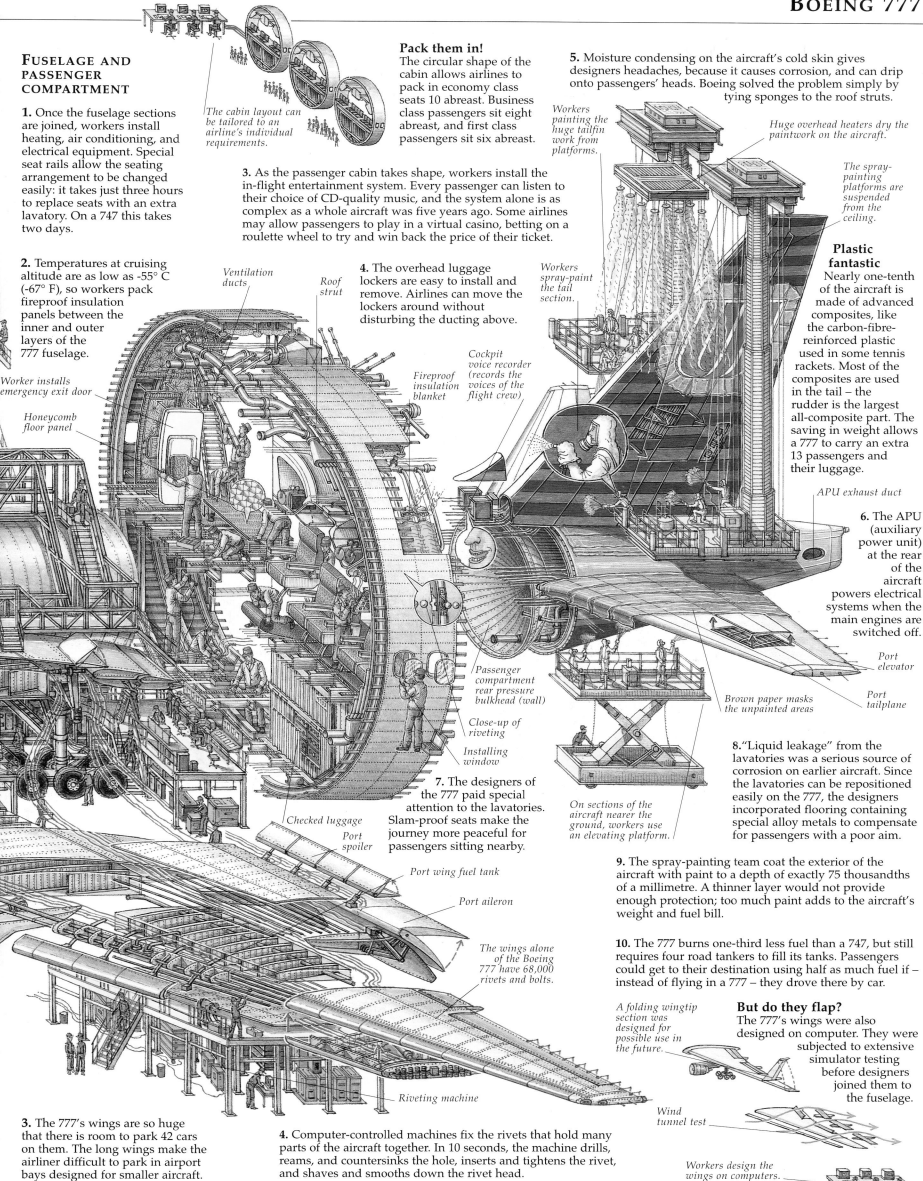

FUSELAGE AND PASSENGER COMPARTMENT

1. Once the fuselage sections are joined, workers install heating, air conditioning, and electrical equipment. Special seat rails allow the seating arrangement to be changed easily: it takes just three hours to replace seats with an extra lavatory. On a 747 this takes two days.

2. Temperatures at cruising altitude are as low as -55° C (-67° F), so workers pack fireproof insulation panels between the inner and outer layers of the 777 fuselage.

The cabin layout can be tailored to an airline's individual requirements.

Pack them in!
The circular shape of the cabin allows airlines to pack in economy class seats 10 abreast. Business class passengers sit eight abreast, and first class passengers sit six abreast.

3. As the passenger cabin takes shape, workers install the in-flight entertainment system. Every passenger can listen to their choice of CD-quality music, and the system alone is as complex as a whole aircraft was five years ago. Some airlines may allow passengers to play in a virtual casino, betting on a roulette wheel to try and win back the price of their ticket.

4. The overhead luggage lockers are easy to install and remove. Airlines can move the lockers around without disturbing the ducting above.

Ventilation ducts

Roof strut

Worker installs emergency exit door

Honeycomb floor panel

Fireproof insulation blanket

Cockpit voice recorder (records the voices of the flight crew)

Passenger compartment rear pressure bulkhead (wall)

Close-up of riveting

Installing window

7. The designers of the 777 paid special attention to the lavatories. Slam-proof seats make the journey more peaceful for passengers sitting nearby.

Checked luggage

Port spoiler

Port wing fuel tank

Port aileron

The wings alone of the Boeing 777 have 68,000 rivets and bolts.

3. The 777's wings are so huge that there is room to park 42 cars on them. The long wings make the airliner difficult to park in airport bays designed for smaller aircraft.

Riveting machine

4. Computer-controlled machines fix the rivets that hold many parts of the aircraft together. In 10 seconds, the machine drills, reams, and countersinks the hole, inserts and tightens the rivet, and shaves and smooths down the rivet head.

5. Moisture condensing on the aircraft's cold skin gives designers headaches, because it causes corrosion, and can drip onto passengers' heads. Boeing solved the problem simply by tying sponges to the roof struts.

Workers painting the huge tailfin work from platforms.

Huge overhead heaters dry the paintwork on the aircraft.

The spray-painting platforms are suspended from the ceiling.

Workers spray-paint the tail section.

Plastic fantastic
Nearly one-tenth of the aircraft is made of advanced composites, like the carbon-fibre-reinforced plastic used in some tennis rackets. Most of the composites are used in the tail – the rudder is the largest all-composite part. The saving in weight allows a 777 to carry an extra 13 passengers and their luggage.

APU exhaust duct

6. The APU (auxiliary power unit) at the rear of the aircraft powers electrical systems when the main engines are switched off.

Port elevator

Port tailplane

Brown paper masks the unpainted areas

On sections of the aircraft nearer the ground, workers use an elevating platform.

8. "Liquid leakage" from the lavatories was a serious source of corrosion on earlier aircraft. Since the lavatories can be repositioned easily on the 777, the designers incorporated flooring containing special alloy metals to compensate for passengers with a poor aim.

9. The spray-painting team coat the exterior of the aircraft with paint to a depth of exactly 75 thousandths of a millimetre. A thinner layer would not provide enough protection; too much paint adds to the aircraft's weight and fuel bill.

10. The 777 burns one-third less fuel than a 747, but still requires four road tankers to fill its tanks. Passengers could get to their destination using half as much fuel if – instead of flying in a 777 – they drove there by car.

A folding wingtip section was designed for possible use in the future.

But do they flap?
The 777's wings were also designed on computer. They were subjected to extensive simulator testing before designers joined them to the fuselage.

Wind tunnel test

Workers design the wings on computers.

SOAP

People began washing with soap only in the second century AD. In earlier times they pounded clothes with earth and urine to clean them.

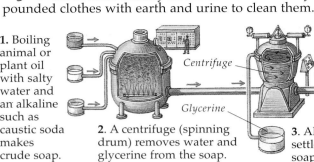

1. Boiling animal or plant oil with salty water and an alkaline such as caustic soda makes crude soap.

Centrifuge

Glycerine

2. A centrifuge (spinning drum) removes water and glycerine from the soap.

Settling tank

3. Allowing the mixture to settle in a tank separates the soap from heavier impurities.

"I like noodles!"

Vacuum dryer

"Mmm!"

5. Compressing the soap squeezes it into a long bar, which a cutter slices into smaller bars.

Colour and perfume are added to the soap noodles.

4. Spraying the liquid soap into a vacuum dries it. Then another machine turns the mixture into noodle-like strands.

Soap is still soft

6. A dryer removes the last of the water.

7. Packing completes the process, which takes a few hours in all. To make soap by hand takes about a week.

Wrapping the bars

Stamping a design onto each bar

ALUMINIUM FOIL

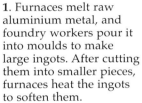

The metal foil we now use to cover leftovers was once as valuable as silver, and used only for jewellery and trinkets.

Cutting ingots

Casting ingots

The hot slab is ready for rolling.

1. Furnaces melt raw aluminium metal, and foundry workers pour it into moulds to make large ingots. After cutting them into smaller pieces, furnaces heat the ingots to soften them.

2. The hot ingot is placed on a conveyor belt, which moves it back and forth between heavy rollers. Workers move the rollers closer together on each pass to create a long slab.

Roller

The ingot moves back and forth between the rollers.

3. Once the slab has cooled, more rollers flatten it into a roll of thin foil. Annealing (heating in a furnace) makes the foil flexible and sterilizes it.

The ingot has now cooled, ready for further rolling.

By the last rolling, the ingots have turned into foil.

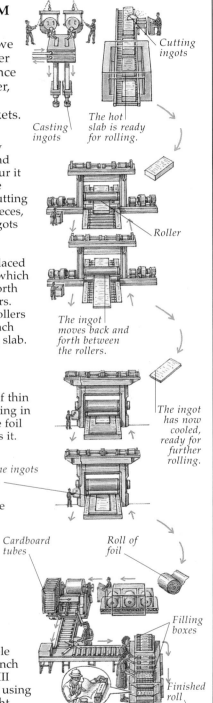

4. Machines wind the foil onto cardboard tubes, and workers pack them into boxes. Other machines shape thicker foil into food containers.

Cardboard tubes

Roll of foil

Filling boxes

Finished roll

"Rats! Foiled again!"

Light load

Aluminium became more widely available after 1854, when French Emperor Napoleon III (1808-73) thought of using it to make lightweight equipment for his army.

NUCLEAR POWER

Splitting an atom releases vast amounts of energy. Just two tiny pellets of uranium fuel can generate one person's annual electricity supply.

Hot gas

Graphite sleeve

Fuel pellet   *Steel can*

Steel case

"Brekkie!"

Graphite control rod

Heat exchanger

1. Uranium dioxide fuel pellets are sealed inside cans, which are stacked in sleeves, which in turn are sealed inside cases. Eight cases make up each fuel rod.

Water turns into steam

A pump recirculates the coolant gas around the reactor core.

Pressure vessel

Pump

The core is sheathed in concrete.

2. When engineers pull out the graphite control rods, a nuclear chain reaction (see below) heats the reactor core. Gas flowing through the core carries heat away.

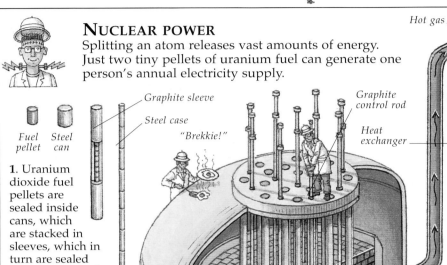

A neutron hits the uranium nucleus.

The nucleus splits and releases two more neutrons.

A domestic transformer reduces the voltage.

"Anything good on?"

Nuclear chain reaction

Atoms of certain materials such as uranium give off tiny particles called neutrons. This is called radioactive decay. The neutrons collide at high speed with the nuclei (centres) of nearby atoms.

The collision causes these atoms to decay in turn, giving off more neutrons. Huge amounts of energy are released as heat. Reactors harvest this energy.

PAPER

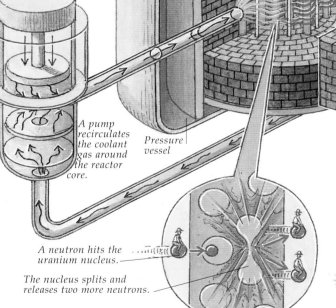

Debarking

Chipping

Paper began replacing parchment (animal skins) in Europe 800 years ago. Most paper today is made from wood pulp.

1. The logs arrive at the factory, and a machine cuts them up into chips. The chips then pass through a digester, which reduces them to stock (fibres and water).

Digester uses steam and heat

Bleacher

Washer

Stock tank

2. The stock spreads from a slot onto a wire belt, draining off excess water.

The stock moves onto a wire belt.

Rollers draw paper over felt blankets.

3. Then the paper begins a long drying process. It passes between heated drums, which drive off most of the surplus water as steam.

Heated drum

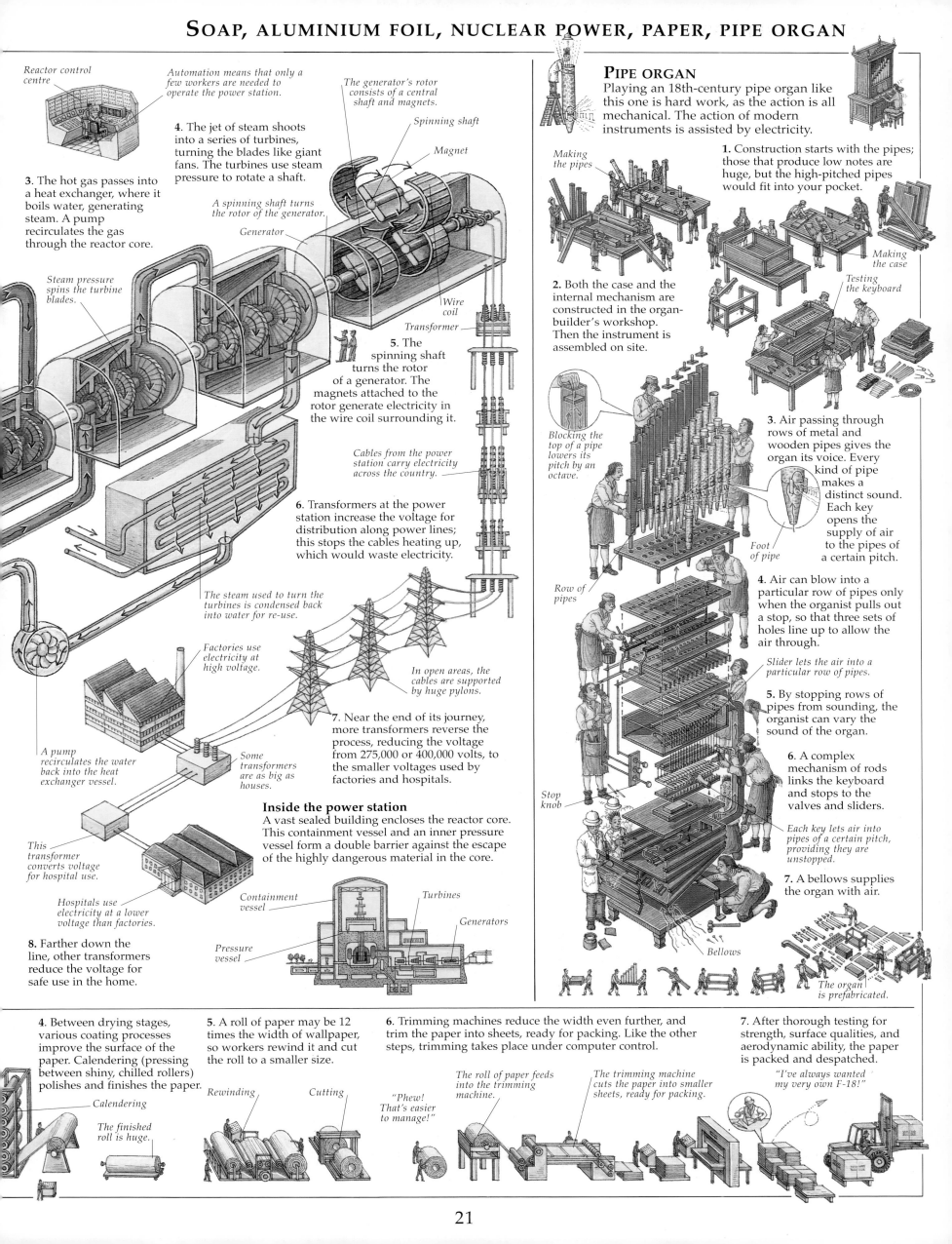

Reactor control centre

Automation means that only a few workers are needed to operate the power station.

The generator's rotor consists of a central shaft and magnets.

Spinning shaft

4. The jet of steam shoots into a series of turbines, turning the blades like giant fans. The turbines use steam pressure to rotate a shaft.

Magnet

3. The hot gas passes into a heat exchanger, where it boils water, generating steam. A pump recirculates the gas through the reactor core.

A spinning shaft turns the rotor of the generator.

Generator

Steam pressure spins the turbine blades.

Wire coil

Transformer

5. The spinning shaft turns the rotor of a generator. The magnets attached to the rotor generate electricity in the wire coil surrounding it.

Cables from the power station carry electricity across the country.

6. Transformers at the power station increase the voltage for distribution along power lines; this stops the cables heating up, which would waste electricity.

The steam used to turn the turbines is condensed back into water for re-use.

Factories use electricity at high voltage.

In open areas, the cables are supported by huge pylons.

7. Near the end of its journey, more transformers reverse the process, reducing the voltage from 275,000 or 400,000 volts, to the smaller voltages used by factories and hospitals.

A pump recirculates the water back into the heat exchanger vessel.

Some transformers are as big as houses.

This transformer converts voltage for hospital use.

Inside the power station
A vast sealed building encloses the reactor core. This containment vessel and an inner pressure vessel form a double barrier against the escape of the highly dangerous material in the core.

Hospitals use electricity at a lower voltage than factories.

8. Farther down the line, other transformers reduce the voltage for safe use in the home.

Containment vessel

Turbines

Generators

Pressure vessel

PIPE ORGAN
Playing an 18th-century pipe organ like this one is hard work, as the action is all mechanical. The action of modern instruments is assisted by electricity.

Making the pipes

1. Construction starts with the pipes; those that produce low notes are huge, but the high-pitched pipes would fit into your pocket.

2. Both the case and the internal mechanism are constructed in the organ-builder's workshop. Then the instrument is assembled on site.

Making the case

Testing the keyboard

Blocking the top of a pipe lowers its pitch by an octave.

3. Air passing through rows of metal and wooden pipes gives the organ its voice. Every kind of pipe makes a distinct sound. Each key opens the supply of air to the pipes of a certain pitch.

Foot of pipe

Row of pipes

4. Air can blow into a particular row of pipes only when the organist pulls out a stop, so that three sets of holes line up to allow the air through.

Slider lets the air into a particular row of pipes.

5. By stopping rows of pipes from sounding, the organist can vary the sound of the organ.

6. A complex mechanism of rods links the keyboard and stops to the valves and sliders.

Stop knob

Each key lets air into pipes of a certain pitch, providing they are unstopped.

7. A bellows supplies the organ with air.

Bellows

The organ is prefabricated.

---

4. Between drying stages, various coating processes improve the surface of the paper. Calendering (pressing between shiny, chilled rollers) polishes and finishes the paper.

Calendering

The finished roll is huge.

5. A roll of paper may be 12 times the width of wallpaper, so workers rewind it and cut the roll to a smaller size.

Rewinding

Cutting

6. Trimming machines reduce the width even further, and trim the paper into sheets, ready for packing. Like the other steps, trimming takes place under computer control.

"Phew! That's easier to manage!"

The roll of paper feeds into the trimming machine.

The trimming machine cuts the paper into smaller sheets, ready for packing.

7. After thorough testing for strength, surface qualities, and aerodynamic ability, the paper is packed and despatched.

"I've always wanted my very own F-18!"

RACING CAR

COMPARING A FORMULA 1 RACING CAR TO A family saloon is like comparing an outfit from a high-street chain store to a gown from a top fashion designer. Every aspect of a racing car is made to measure. The cockpit fits around the driver's body like a tight pair of jeans so drivers have to watch their weight just like a supermodel. The first Formula 1 race of the year is in many ways like a fashion show. Everyone stares at the new cars, examining every detail and watching how the design affects each car's performance on the track.

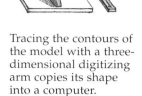

THE DESIGN
Designers aim to make the body light but strong. Its shape helps the car grip the track.

Working from the drawings, a team of modelmakers sculpt the body shape in miniature.

Tracing the contours of the model with a three-dimensional digitizing arm copies its shape into a computer.

THE BODY OF THE CAR
The shape of a car's body has a huge effect on speed, so designers decide this first. Engineers must then find room for all the car's other components – such as the engine and suspension – in the tiny body. To give all cars an equal chance, strict rules govern every construction detail.

1. One of the biggest dangers to drivers is a fuel fire. A quarter of the car's weight when the race starts is highly flammable fuel, and drivers sit in front of the tank. Shock-absorbing panels protect it, and a puncture-resistant bladder stops fuel leaking in a crash.

2. On a saloon car, the suspension smooths the ride. On a racing car, it must stop the car bouncing up, as this reduces the wheel's grip on the track. Bump-detecting sensors feed information to a central computer that operates the hydraulic jacks controlling the height of each wheel. The basic layout of the suspension is easy to modify at the track by adjusting the car's computer.

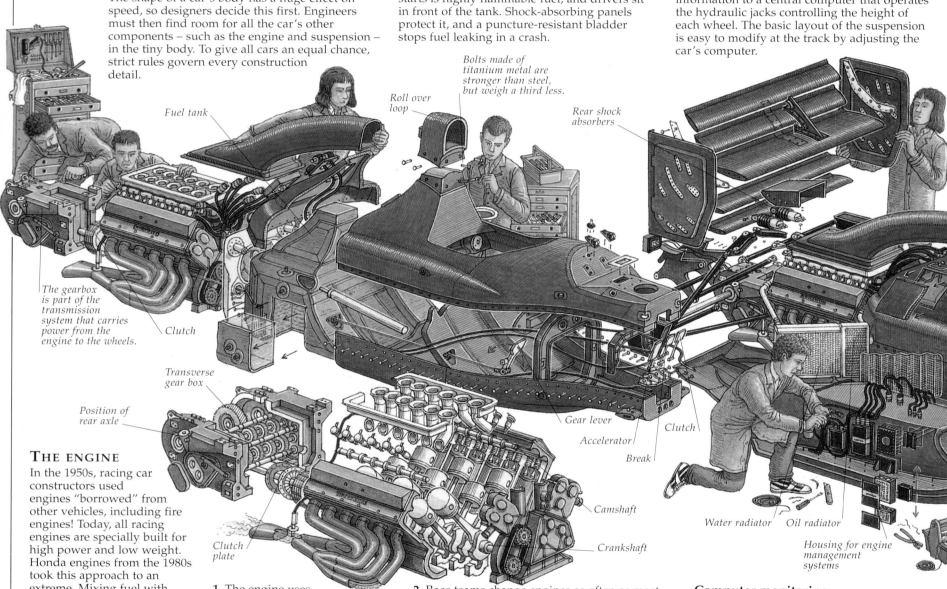

Fuel tank

Bolts made of titanium metal are stronger than steel, but weigh a third less.

Roll over loop

Rear shock absorbers

The gearbox is part of the transmission system that carries power from the engine to the wheels.

Clutch

Transverse gear box

Position of rear axle

Gear lever

Accelerator

Break

Clutch

Camshaft

Crankshaft

Clutch plate

Water radiator *Oil radiator*

Housing for engine management systems

THE ENGINE
In the 1950s, racing car constructors used engines "borrowed" from other vehicles, including fire engines! Today, all racing engines are specially built for high power and low weight. Honda engines from the 1980s took this approach to an extreme. Mixing fuel with compressed air, their engines generated 20 times as much power as a saloon car engine of the same size.

1. The engine uses less than a third of all the fuel it burns to move the car round the track. More is wasted in noise and heat from the exhaust.

2. Race teams change engines as often as most people change their underwear. After each race, mechanics dismantle the car, remove the engine and ship it back to the manufacturers. The engine may be re-used the following season, but it is often replaced by a newer, faster model.

Computer monitoring
Sensors all over the car monitor its performance, and an on-board computer stores the information. Technicians collect the information during a pit-stop, or the car broadcasts a short burst of data by radio.

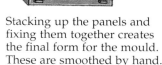

BUILDING THE BODY
A computer-controlled milling machine cuts moulds for the body from flat panels.

Stacking up the panels and fixing them together creates the final form for the mould. These are smoothed by hand.

Fabricators first paint over release agents and wax to prevent sticking, and then coat the form with epoxy resin.

Next the form is carefully covered with around ten layers of carbon fibre sheeting. This is the mould.

To strengthen the body, it is "cured" in an oven at 120° C (250° F) – just hot enough to cook meringues.

On the computer, engineers can plan how the body will fit together with other components. The computer model will also guide cutters that make moulds for the full-sized car.

To simulate a race, a huge fan blows air across the model in a wind tunnel, and an endless belt turns the wheels. Sensors measure drag, down-force, and vibration. These tests help predict how the car will behave on the track.

While the fan is switched off, engineers run into the tunnel and change tiny details of the car. They have to hurry, because wind tunnel time is very expensive.

Modifications that improve the flow of air over the model will make the full-sized car go faster.

THE "CLOTHES" OF THE CAR

The flaps, spoilers, and tyres are like the racing car's clothes. Engineers decide on the basic outfit at the design stage. But many of these parts are easy to remove. The pit crew exchanges them to make small adjustments to the car's performance. The spoilers work like an upside-down aircraft wing. The faster the car goes, the more it is pressed to the ground, improving the grip of the tyres.

THE FINISHING TOUCHES

Finishing touches include a shiny paint finish and advertising for sponsors – companies that give money to racing teams in exchange for publicity. The more money a sponsor provides, the larger and more prominent their logo appears on the car. The technicians must position the company logos carefully to keep all the sponsors happy.

THE DRIVER

Drivers wear fireproof clothes made of multiple layers of high-temperature-resistant nylon. If there's a fire, the suit keeps out the flames for half a minute. An emergency canister supplies compressed air to the helmet, preventing drivers from suffocating or breathing in poisonous fumes. The eye-slit of the fireproof glass-fibre-reinforced helmet is narrow to protect against flying debris.

Spoilers (wings) at the front and back create a downward force that is greater than the car's weight.

Six-point harness

The seat is not padded and the driver feels every bump.

Epaulettes are reinforced so the driver can be dragged from a burning wreck.

"Even his underwear is flame resistant!"

Brake pads

The housings for the brakes are designed to channel air across the discs to cool them. As drivers brake, the carbon-fibre discs glow red hot. They work best at 350-500⁰ C (660-930⁰ F).

The nose is designed to crumple and absorb shock on impact.

The chassis of the car is made up of two layers of carbon fibre, with either an aluminium honeycomb structure or a flame-resistant material called "Nomex" in the middle.

Race teams use many different tyres, changing them for different circuits and different weather.

Spoiler

Technicians monitor data on the car's performance.

PIT STOP

During a race, cars call in at the pits (small workshops) for refuelling, new tyres, data download, and other maintenance. A team of up to 50 mechanics and technicians work at dizzying speed to get the car back into the race as quickly as possible. With three mechanics on each wheel, changing all four tyres takes ten seconds or less.

Rear left wheel mechanics

Refuellers

Front left wheel mechanics

Rear quick-lift jack operator

Front quick-lift jack operator

Most cars are made from five mouldings or fewer. During assembly, technicians add aluminium bulkheads to strengthen the cockpit.

Before a new car can race, it must pass stringent safety tests and survive simulated side and front impacts.

"Right, let's try it again with you in the driving seat."

Rear right wheel mechanics

Front right wheel mechanics

Chief mechanic with the lollipop for signalling to the driver

GUNPOWDER

Old-fashioned explosive gunpowder was made from three elements: 10 parts sulphur, 15 parts charcoal, and 75 parts saltpetre (potassium nitrate).

Sulphur *Making charcoal* *Pile of compost*

Refining sulphur *Refining saltpetre*

1. Yellow brimstone (sulphur) was taken from volcanoes. Pure sulphur crackles if you hold it to your ear.

2. Charcoal is made by burning wood without air. A fire was covered with turfs to do this.

3. Saltpetre came from nitrogen-rich soils and animal dung. The king's saltpetre men collected it from barns.

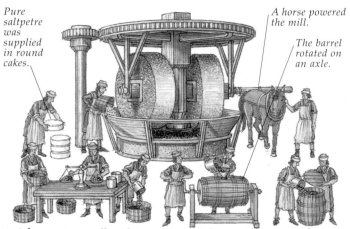

Pure saltpetre was supplied in round cakes.

A horse powered the mill.

The barrel rotated on an axle.

4. A huge stone roller, driven by horse or water power, crushed the cakes of purified saltpetre into a fine powder.

5. After weighing out the ingredients, workers tumbled them in a barrel to mix them.

6. The most dangerous step was incorporation. This process mixed the ingredients and milled them into grains.

Accidents were common with such a dangerous explosive substance.

7. Water-powered pestles pounded the mixture once each second. This process took 24 hours.

8. The finished gunpowder grains were now highly explosive. Workers stored them carefully.

Corning *Tumbling*

9. Corning (forcing the powder through holes in a parchment sheet) then tumbling it in a barrel produced larger pellets of explosive.

10. To prevent an explosion, the powder dried in a "gloom stove" – a room heated by the back of a fire burning next door.

Gentle heat dried the powder safely.

Powder sat on the racks in the room.

"Stand clear!" *"Fire!"* *"Looks good!"*

11. Good gunpowder burned cleanly, and did not ignite another heap of powder a hand's-width away.

12. Gunpowder was also tested with a cannon, and the penetration of the shot was measured.

WIG

Wig thieves flourished in crowded 18th-century streets. Sitting on a man's shoulders, a small boy snatched the fashionable wigs from passing heads. Modern wig-wearers face no similar perils!

1. A tailor-made wig needs careful measuring if it is to fit properly and look like real hair.

The foundation rests on a block. *The wig is ready for styling.*

Foundation

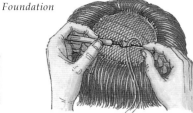

2. The wigmaker crafts a nylon cap, called a foundation, to hold all the hair in place.

3. The wigmaker knots up to 150,000 hairs individually along a parting.

4. While the wig is being made, it rests on a head-shaped block. The finished wig has long hair.

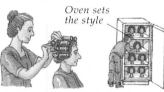

Oven sets the style

5. Back in the salon, the hairdresser cuts and styles the wig as if it was the wearer's real hair.

6. To create curly hair, the hairdresser uses rollers, then sets the style in a cool oven.

7. Elastic and adhesive tape hold the wig in position – even in a gale!

CATHEDRAL

Medieval masons created spectacular cathedrals using simple hand tools. The spire of Strasbourg is the height of a 44-storey office block; Amiens Cathedral is so vast that everyone in the city could worship together when it was completed.

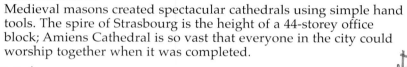

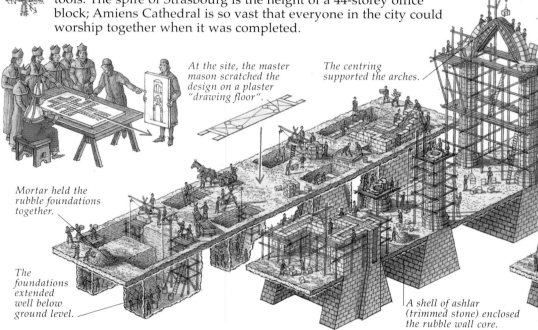

At the site, the master mason scratched the design on a plaster "drawing floor".

The centring supported the arches.

Mortar held the rubble foundations together.

The foundations extended well below ground level.

A shell of ashlar (trimmed stone) enclosed the rubble wall core.

1. The master mason (architect) presented drawings on parchment to show roughly what the building would look like.

2. Workers built the cathedral foundations on solid bedrock, sometimes digging down 10-15 m (33-50 ft).

3. Carpenters built wooden centring as temporary supports for the stone arches. Masons cut stones on the ground to fit.

BRICK

Bricks were all handmade until about 1860. Now they are made in factories by machines.

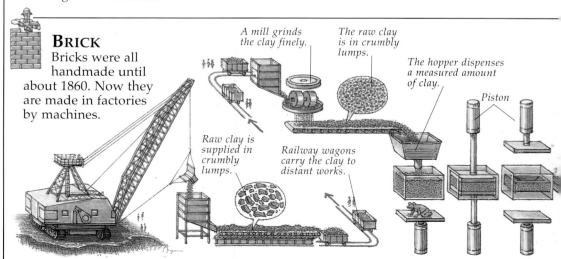

A mill grinds the clay finely.

The raw clay is in crumbly lumps.

The hopper dispenses a measured amount of clay.

Piston

Raw clay is supplied in crumbly lumps.

Railway wagons carry the clay to distant works.

1. A shovel excavator digs out the raw materials (clay or shale) for the bricks.

2. A conveyor belt or train moves the clay from the quarry to the brickworks.

3. Pistons press the semi-dry clay into a brick-shaped mould, compacting it.

A lead weight
The lead covering the roof of the cathedral was often the most valuable part of the whole building. The amount of metal on a roof could be huge. During the Great Fire of London in 1666, the roof of Old St. Paul's Cathedral melted and sent a river of molten lead flowing through the streets.

Masons used ladders and scaffolding to reach their work.

"Hmm, this looks like it will hold for a few centuries!"

Lead sheeting protected the wooden roof against rain.

Buttresses prevented the walls from splaying out under the weight of the lead roof.

Wooden scaffolding

Slender columns allowed for big windows of coloured glass.

Winch lifts stones

Layer of concrete

Vault rib

The mosaic floor maze was for worship: the faithful traced the winding path on their knees.

It's all your vault...
Vaults were the only way medieval masons could construct a large ceiling area. Only the thick stone ribs needed wooden supports during construction.

1. Masons built the ribs of the vault first.

2. Pieces of wood held up the stones while the mortar between them set.

3. Flat stones were added to create a lightweight ceiling.

4. Finally, a layer of concrete covered the entire vault to seal it.

SPORTS SHOE
Developing the design for a new sports shoe takes many years. Only after extensive research and modifications will the shoe go on sale to the public.

"I think it needs a thicker sole."

1. The athletes who will use the shoe are consulted at the design stage.

Trim
Upper
Finished sample shoe
Sole
Cushion
Sole insert

2. A sample shoe is built. Most sports shoes have five main parts, but there may be many more.

"Pooh! We need to work on the ventilation!"
"It runs by itself!"

3. Field trials are carried out.

Cutting pieces of leather
Sewing machine

4. The shoes are assembled mainly by hand. Workers stitch the uppers and trim, then glue the soles to the uppers.

"Glad we got that ventilation fixed!"

5. The quality of the finished shoes is carefully checked.

Building many identical bays extended the cathedral's length.

4. Masons completed work on one bay (the section between two main columns) before starting the next. Building work stopped in winter, and thatch covered uncompleted walls to prevent damage by rain and frost.

5. Construction of the vaults (arched stone ceilings) was the trickiest part of the entire building job. Carpenters constructed a temporary roof, so that masons could then work on the first stage of the vaults protected from the weather.

6. Once the roof was covered with lead, the vaults could be finished, and the floor of the cathedral laid. Last of all, the interior was decorated.

7. Building a cathedral took so long that the architect was often dead by the time the cathedral opened. Some cathedrals took hundreds of years to complete.

The indentation pressed into each side of the brick to hold the mortar is called the "frog".

Warm air

Machinery does much of the back-breaking work in the factory.

Kiln workers wear clogs to protect their feet.

"Ow! That's hot!"

Cars loaded with bricks move through the kiln, which never cools.

Bricks are unloaded and sorted by type and colour.

Roller adds texture

Dye spray

Kiln door

4. Machine-made bricks look uniform. A bumpy roller adds a "handmade" texture, and dye is sprayed on to colour the brick.

5. The bricks are then dried. Warm air circulates around the bricks – drawing off moisture.

6. A setting machine loads the bricks onto a small car.

7. Heating in a kiln hardens the clay bricks to a stone-like texture.

8. After cooling, another machine unloads the bricks for sorting and packing.

INCREDIBLE EVERYTHING

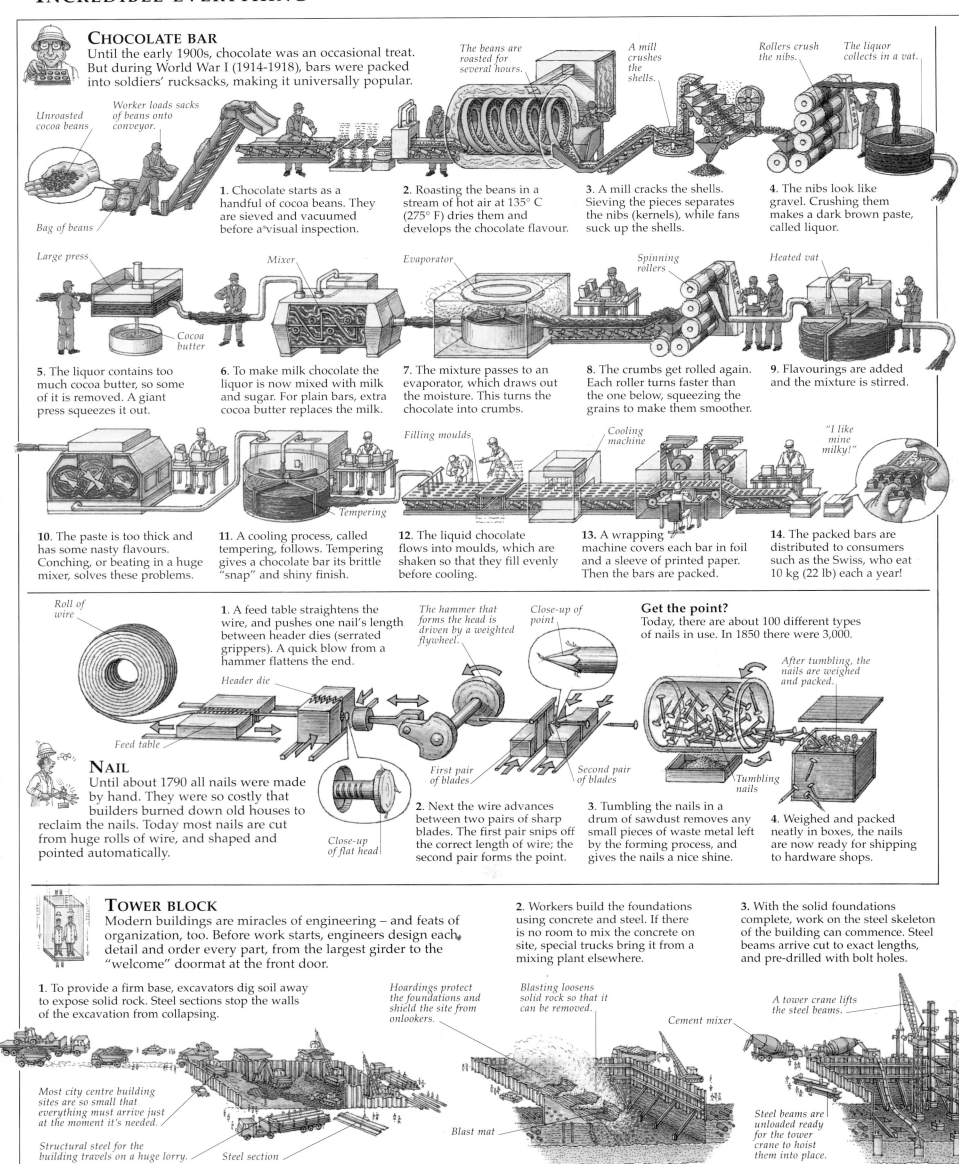

CHOCOLATE BAR

Until the early 1900s, chocolate was an occasional treat. But during World War I (1914-1918), bars were packed into soldiers' rucksacks, making it universally popular.

Unroasted cocoa beans

Worker loads sacks of beans onto conveyor.

Bag of beans

The beans are roasted for several hours.

A mill crushes the shells.

Rollers crush the nibs.

The liquor collects in a vat.

1. Chocolate starts as a handful of cocoa beans. They are sieved and vacuumed before a visual inspection.

2. Roasting the beans in a stream of hot air at 135° C (275° F) dries them and develops the chocolate flavour.

3. A mill cracks the shells. Sieving the pieces separates the nibs (kernels), while fans suck up the shells.

4. The nibs look like gravel. Crushing them makes a dark brown paste, called liquor.

Large press *Mixer* *Evaporator* *Spinning rollers* *Heated vat*

Cocoa butter

5. The liquor contains too much cocoa butter, so some of it is removed. A giant press squeezes it out.

6. To make milk chocolate the liquor is now mixed with milk and sugar. For plain bars, extra cocoa butter replaces the milk.

7. The mixture passes to an evaporator, which draws out the moisture. This turns the chocolate into crumbs.

8. The crumbs get rolled again. Each roller turns faster than the one below, squeezing the grains to make them smoother.

9. Flavourings are added and the mixture is stirred.

Filling moulds *Cooling machine* *"I like mine milky!"*

Tempering

10. The paste is too thick and has some nasty flavours. Conching, or beating in a huge mixer, solves these problems.

11. A cooling process, called tempering, follows. Tempering gives a chocolate bar its brittle "snap" and shiny finish.

12. The liquid chocolate flows into moulds, which are shaken so that they fill evenly before cooling.

13. A wrapping machine covers each bar in foil and a sleeve of printed paper. Then the bars are packed.

14. The packed bars are distributed to consumers such as the Swiss, who eat 10 kg (22 lb) each a year!

Roll of wire

1. A feed table straightens the wire, and pushes one nail's length between header dies (serrated grippers). A quick blow from a hammer flattens the end.

The hammer that forms the head is driven by a weighted flywheel.

Close-up of point

Get the point?
Today, there are about 100 different types of nails in use. In 1850 there were 3,000.

After tumbling, the nails are weighed and packed.

Header die

Feed table

Close-up of flat head

First pair of blades

Second pair of blades

Tumbling nails

NAIL

Until about 1790 all nails were made by hand. They were so costly that builders burned down old houses to reclaim the nails. Today most nails are cut from huge rolls of wire, and shaped and pointed automatically.

2. Next the wire advances between two pairs of sharp blades. The first pair snips off the correct length of wire; the second pair forms the point.

3. Tumbling the nails in a drum of sawdust removes any small pieces of waste metal left by the forming process, and gives the nails a nice shine.

4. Weighed and packed neatly in boxes, the nails are now ready for shipping to hardware shops.

TOWER BLOCK

Modern buildings are miracles of engineering – and feats of organization, too. Before work starts, engineers design each detail and order every part, from the largest girder to the "welcome" doormat at the front door.

2. Workers build the foundations using concrete and steel. If there is no room to mix the concrete on site, special trucks bring it from a mixing plant elsewhere.

3. With the solid foundations complete, work on the steel skeleton of the building can commence. Steel beams arrive cut to exact lengths, and pre-drilled with bolt holes.

1. To provide a firm base, excavators dig soil away to expose solid rock. Steel sections stop the walls of the excavation from collapsing.

Hoardings protect the foundations and shield the site from onlookers.

Blasting loosens solid rock so that it can be removed.

A tower crane lifts the steel beams.

Cement mixer

Most city centre building sites are so small that everything must arrive just at the moment it's needed.

Structural steel for the building travels on a huge lorry.

Steel section

Blast mat

Steel beams are unloaded ready for the tower crane to hoist them into place.

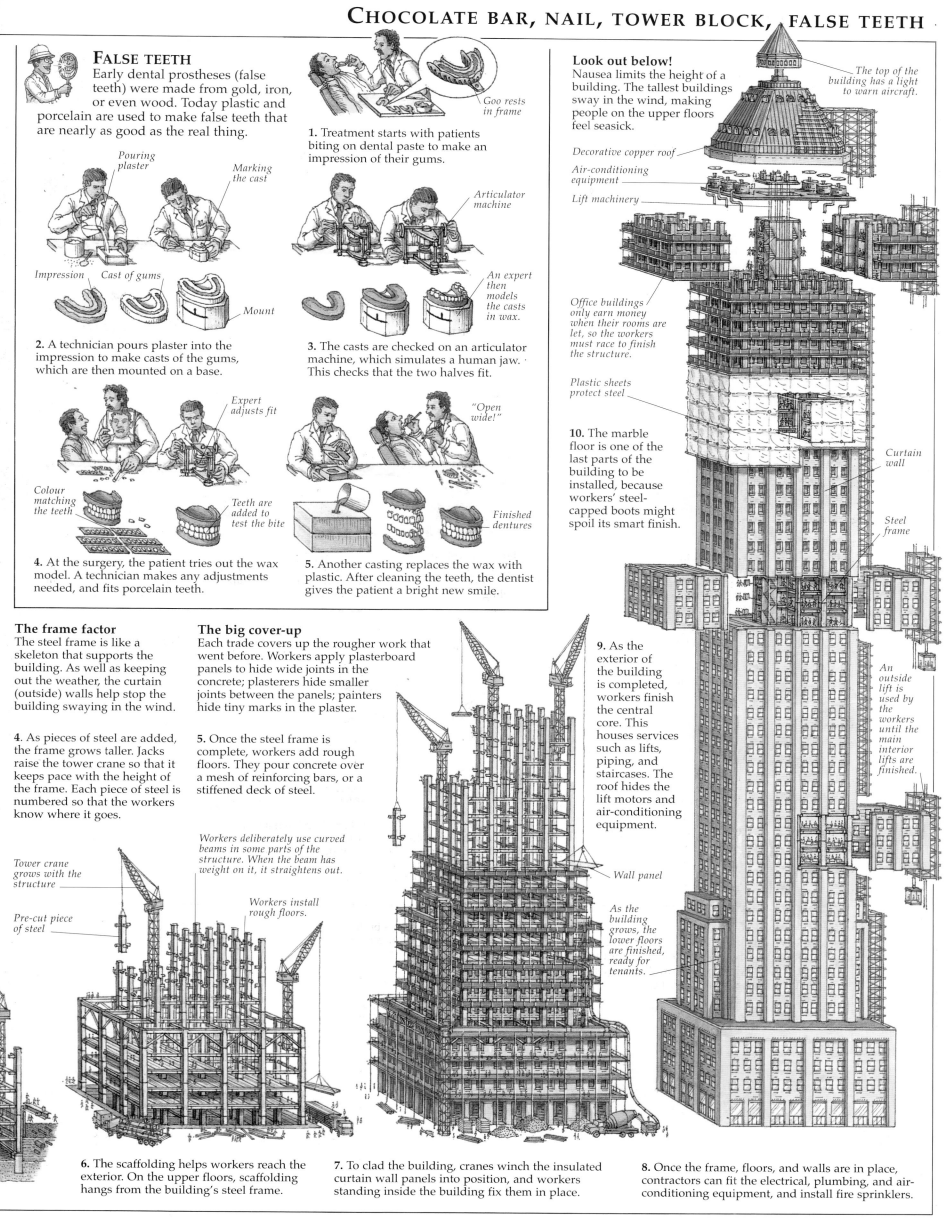

FALSE TEETH

Early dental prostheses (false teeth) were made from gold, iron, or even wood. Today plastic and porcelain are used to make false teeth that are nearly as good as the real thing.

Goo rests in frame

1. Treatment starts with patients biting on dental paste to make an impression of their gums.

Pouring plaster

Marking the cast

Impression   *Cast of gums*

Mount

2. A technician pours plaster into the impression to make casts of the gums, which are then mounted on a base.

Articulator machine

An expert then models the casts in wax.

3. The casts are checked on an articulator machine, which simulates a human jaw. This checks that the two halves fit.

Expert adjusts fit

Colour matching the teeth

Teeth are added to test the bite

4. At the surgery, the patient tries out the wax model. A technician makes any adjustments needed, and fits porcelain teeth.

"Open wide!"

Finished dentures

5. Another casting replaces the wax with plastic. After cleaning the teeth, the dentist gives the patient a bright new smile.

Look out below!

Nausea limits the height of a building. The tallest buildings sway in the wind, making people on the upper floors feel seasick.

The top of the building has a light to warn aircraft.

Decorative copper roof

Air-conditioning equipment

Lift machinery

Office buildings only earn money when their rooms are let, so the workers must race to finish the structure.

Plastic sheets protect steel

10. The marble floor is one of the last parts of the building to be installed, because workers' steel-capped boots might spoil its smart finish.

Curtain wall

Steel frame

9. As the exterior of the building is completed, workers finish the central core. This houses services such as lifts, piping, and staircases. The roof hides the lift motors and air-conditioning equipment.

An outside lift is used by the workers until the main interior lifts are finished.

The frame factor

The steel frame is like a skeleton that supports the building. As well as keeping out the weather, the curtain (outside) walls help stop the building swaying in the wind.

4. As pieces of steel are added, the frame grows taller. Jacks raise the tower crane so that it keeps pace with the height of the frame. Each piece of steel is numbered so that the workers know where it goes.

The big cover-up

Each trade covers up the rougher work that went before. Workers apply plasterboard panels to hide wide joints in the concrete; plasterers hide smaller joints between the panels; painters hide tiny marks in the plaster.

5. Once the steel frame is complete, workers add rough floors. They pour concrete over a mesh of reinforcing bars, or a stiffened deck of steel.

Workers deliberately use curved beams in some parts of the structure. When the beam has weight on it, it straightens out.

Tower crane grows with the structure

Pre-cut piece of steel

Workers install rough floors.

Wall panel

As the building grows, the lower floors are finished, ready for tenants.

6. The scaffolding helps workers reach the exterior. On the upper floors, scaffolding hangs from the building's steel frame.

7. To clad the building, cranes winch the insulated curtain wall panels into position, and workers standing inside the building fix them in place.

8. Once the frame, floors, and walls are in place, contractors can fit the electrical, plumbing, and air-conditioning equipment, and install fire sprinklers.

DAILY NEWSPAPER

"READALLABOUTIT" SHOUTS THE NEWSPAPER seller. When earthquakes strike or wars break out, we want to read the news in our daily paper as soon as it happens, or preferably sooner! Filling newspapers with eyewitness reports and dramatic pictures is a challenge almost as demanding as predicting the future. To collect stories, journalists and photographers travel all over the world, often to dangerous places. The stories are then sent or taken to the newspaper offices, where a team processes the information to create pages on computer terminals. At a printing site, the pages are converted into negative film from which a printing plate is produced. Many newspapers worldwide are run out on a press like this one, where a large roll of paper, or web, is used in a continuous printing process. Now read on!

Satellite links allow journalists to send in stories from almost anywhere.

When a story arrives at a newspaper, it is routed to the correct desk by computer.

Where possible, reporters return to the newspaper's offices to file their stories, and many journalists work there on background or information articles called features.

Sometimes journalists type their news stories straight onto laptop computers, and send, or "file", them directly with a newspaper by telephone line or by satellite phone.

Many newspapers keep their selling price down by earning money from advertising. Sales staff sell space in the newspaper, taking down details by phone.

NEWS GATHERING
Reporters and photographers travel the country to collect news. Only the larger papers can afford to send journalists abroad to report on international events.

Much foreign news comes from news agencies that employ journalists and photographers worldwide. The agency operates a telephone wire service to send a story to a newspaper.

In the newsroom, sub-editors, picture editors, and designers lay out each page of the newspaper on computer terminals. Large screens show them how each page will look.

Every day, departmental chiefs of a newspaper meet with the editor to discuss the day's news stories. Together they decide which stories and pictures to include in the following day's newspaper.

News happens 24 hours a day, and the night editor has to be ready to make changes right through the night – up until the moment when printing starts in the early hours of the morning.

"My truth detector can spot a liar," says Chester.

PLATEMAKING
For each page, four separate printing plates are made, one for each colour (see below). Technicians first create a copy of the page on clear film in an image-setter. This is passed to a processor that develops the film, creating a negative. In an exposure unit, the film is brought into contact with an aluminium plate coated with a special emulsion. Light shining through the film causes chemical changes in the emulsion. Areas struck by light become greasy so ink will stick to them.

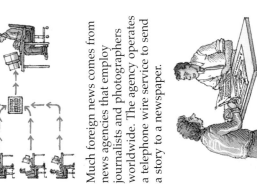

Image setter

Processor

Exposure unit

A machine dries the finished plate

Printing plates are thin enough to wrap around cylinders inside the press.

PRINTING IN COLOUR
The paper runs through four units of the press. These are almost identical – the only difference between them is that each prints a different colour. The first unit prints the cyan (blue) parts of pictures; the second, the magenta (purple) areas; the third, the yellow areas; and the final unit at the top of the press prints the black areas and the black type. By varying the intensity of these four colours, it is possible to create every colour of the rainbow.

THE PRINTING PRESS
When it reaches the printing press, the web runs through the four different colour units. A printing plate is fixed to one of the rollers in each unit, while other rollers transfer ink from a feed trough. Access points everywhere in the press allow technicians to reach inside for maintenance and adjustment

The fourth set of rollers prints both sides with the final colour of the process – black.

FOLDING AND CUTTING
After printing, the paper reaches the top of the press. It runs over rollers that direct the web back down again into the folder. The first blade slits the paper in two, then each half passes through a pair of forming rollers that fold it down the middle. Blades cut the paper and the collecting cylinder puts in more folds. The assembled newspaper drops into a paddle-wheel assembly, which then drops the whole thing onto a delivery belt.

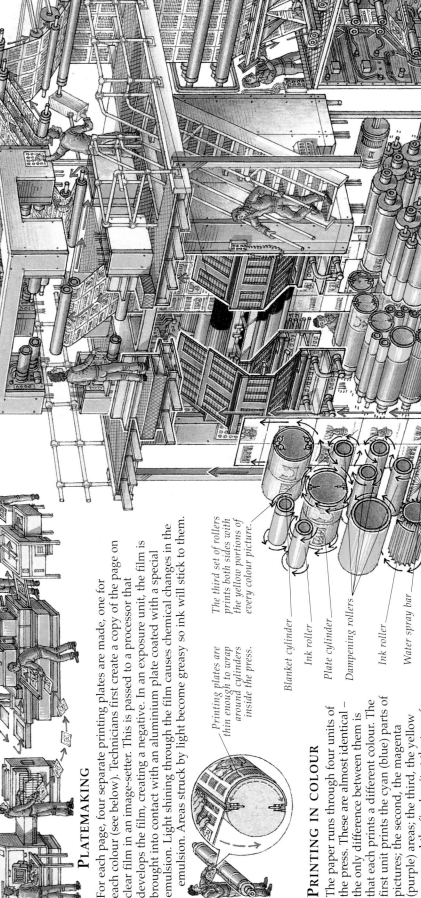

Forming rollers

Folding knife and collecting cylinder

Clips fix the newspapers to an endless chain that carries the papers to packing points.

The third set of rollers prints both sides with the yellow portions of every colour picture.

Blanket cylinder

Ink roller

Plate cylinder

Dampening rollers

Ink roller

Water spray bar

Ink feed

Ink trough

Ink pump

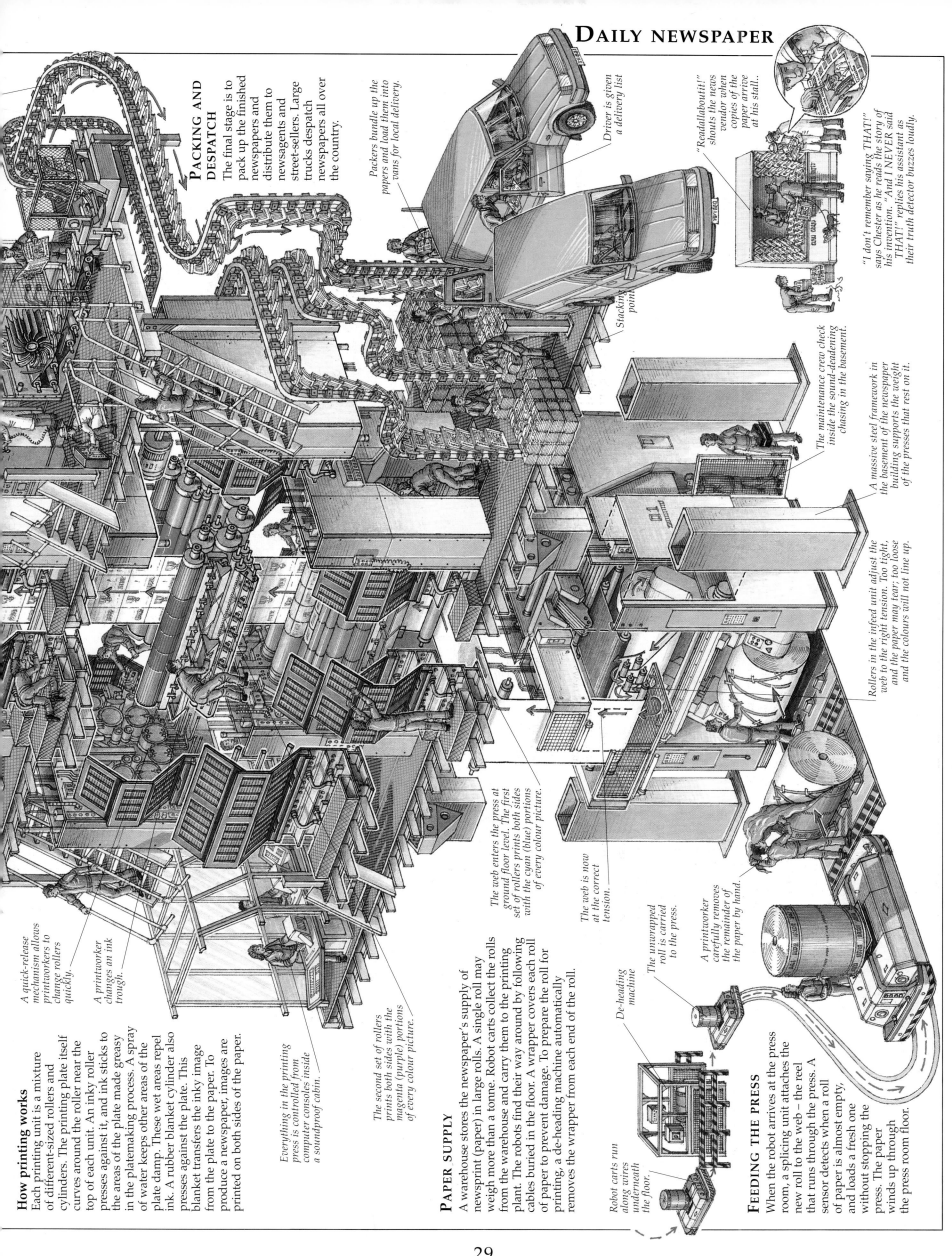

DAILY NEWSPAPER

PACKING AND DESPATCH

The final stage is to pack up the finished newspapers and distribute them to newsagents and street-sellers. Large trucks despatch newspapers all over the country.

Packers bundle up the papers and load them into vans for local delivery.

Driver is given a delivery list.

Stacking point

"Readallaboutit!" shouts the news vendor when copies of the paper arrive at his stall.

"I don't remember saying THAT!" says Chester as he reads the story of his invention. "And I NEVER said THAT!" replies his assistant as their truth detector buzzes loudly.

The maintenance crew check inside the sound-deadening casing in the basement.

A massive steel framework in the basement of the newspaper building supports the weight of the presses that rest on it.

Rollers in the infeed unit adjust the web to the right tension. Too tight, and the paper may tear; too loose and the colours will not line up.

How printing works

Each printing unit is a mixture of different-sized rollers and cylinders. The printing plate itself curves around the roller near the top of each unit. An inky roller presses against it, and ink sticks to the areas of the plate made greasy in the platemaking process. A spray of water keeps other areas of the plate damp. These wet areas repel ink. A rubber blanket cylinder also presses against the plate. This blanket transfers the inky image from the plate to the paper. To produce a newspaper, images are printed on both sides of the paper.

A quick-release mechanism allows printworkers to change rollers quickly.

A printworker changes an ink trough.

Everything in the printing press is controlled from computer consoles inside a soundproof cabin.

The second set of rollers prints both sides with the magenta (purple) portions of every colour picture.

The web enters the press at ground floor level. The first set of rollers prints both sides with the cyan (blue) portions of every colour picture.

The web is now at the correct tension.

The unwrapped roll is carried to the press.

A printworker carefully removes the remainder of the paper by hand.

PAPER SUPPLY

A warehouse stores the newspaper's supply of newsprint (paper) in large rolls. A single roll may weigh more than a tonne. Robot carts collect the rolls from the warehouse and carry them to the printing plant. The robots find their way around by following cables buried in the floor. A wrapper covers each roll of paper to prevent damage. To prepare the roll for printing, a de-heading machine automatically removes the wrapper from each end of the roll.

De-heading machine

Robot carts run along wires underneath the floor.

FEEDING THE PRESS

When the robot arrives at the press room, a splicing unit attaches the new roll to the web – the reel that runs through the press. A sensor detects when a roll of paper is almost empty, and loads a fresh one without stopping the press. The paper winds up through the press room floor.

29

PHOTOCOPY

Introduced in 1949, the first photocopier was slow. Fourteen manual operations were needed to make a copy. Today's copiers use the same principles, but are much quicker.

At the heart of the copier is a revolving, electrically charged drum that attracts black toner dust.

Copying glass

"Smmaack!"

The drum presses the paper against the toner.

Heated roller

"I know...I'll slip in a photograph of my girlfriend Esther!"

Static electricity

The image is projected onto the drum.

1. Static electricity charges the drum's surface. Copying projects an image of the document onto the drum, causing light areas to lose their charge.

Toner image

Drum

Paper exit

Paper feed roller

3. The paper has an opposite charge to the toner, so it attracts the black dust in a pattern that exactly matches the dark areas of the original document.

Toner deposited on the drum

Paper feeds in

Revolving drum

2. Dark areas stay charged and attract toner dust. Then the drum revolves, drawing in paper and pressing it against the toner image.

The lamp erases the image on the drum.

A heated roller fuses the toner.

Exit roller

"AAARGH! WHO is that!"

"Get a move on!"

"Hurry up!"

Brushes remove the surplus toner from the drum.

"Grrr! My tie!"

4. Passing the paper between a pair of heated rollers fuses (melts) the image permanently into the paper.

5. Today's copiers are fast and reliable – and pressing a single "print" button makes "a perfect copy every time!"

MUMMY

The ancient Egyptians preserved people's bodies so their souls could inhabit them in the afterlife. The method they used, called mummification, involved removing the insides and treating the body with chemicals. Only wealthy people could be mummified because the process was very costly.

Animals were mummified too.

1. The embalmers began by scooping out the brains through the nose using special hooks and spoons.

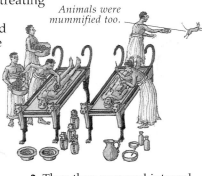

2. They then removed internal organs such as the heart, lungs and liver, and washed the body in spiced palm wine.

Bags of natron

3. To dry and preserve the corpse, it was packed in natron (naturally occurring sodium carbonate).

Some workers washed the body.

Others packed things inside and treated the skin.

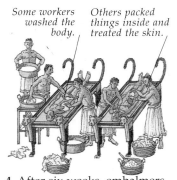

4. After six weeks, embalmers washed it again, and packed linen, sawdust and mud inside. Oil and wax preserved the skin.

The more important people were, the bigger their crowd of mourners.

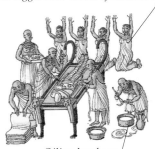

Oiling bandages

5. Twenty layers of strip bandages were carefully dipped in oil, then wound around the corpse.

Canopic jar lids took the shape of human, falcon, dog and jackal heads.

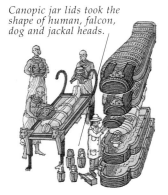

6. A mask with the dead person's features went on the face. The organs were stored in special urns called canopic jars.

UNDERGROUND RAILWAY TUNNEL

Tunnels are dug by boring machines, which are surprisingly interesting. These "moles" cut tunnels or pipelines through soft soil. Only the fastest tunnelling machines dig as quickly as the common mole, which burrows 5.5 m (18 ft) an hour.

The spoil conveyor carries excavated earth from the access shaft to waiting tipper trucks.

Huge fans ventilate the tunnel, and supply air to the workers below the ground.

Ventilation shaft

A stairway provides access to the works below.

TBM guidance laser

Segments bolt together

The completed railway track rests on a concrete bed.

Pouring concrete

Tunnel segment bolt

Base of stairway

Spoil bucket

1. First, an access shaft is dug to the depth of the tunnel. The access shaft is wide because there must be enough space to lower the tunnel-boring machine (TBM) down it. When construction is complete, the shaft provides ventilation for the railway system.

2. Workers build a lining of iron or concrete to stop the shaft collapsing and to keep out water. Then the TBM is lowered to the bottom.

3. Once the TBM is lowered down the shaft, workers begin to use it to dig the tunnel. Mine cars running on temporary track carry spoil (excavated soil) to the foot of the access shaft.

4. At the foot of the shaft, workers empty the spoil into a bucket for removal by crane. Some tunnels use conveyors to remove spoil up a sloping shaft.

5. The TBM is laser-guided. The operator knows the tunnel is straight when a laser hits the target ahead.

6. Scrapers fixed to a rotating cutting wheel on the front of the TBM actually dig the tunnel. Earth falls through the wheel's "spokes" onto a conveyor belt.

DINOSAUR SKELETON

Scientists who excavate fossilized dinosaur bones need the muscles of a construction worker, and the brains of a detective.

Bones can be hidden deep in solid rock, so a road drill and crane can be useful.

No palaeontologist would repeat the errors of the past, and mount a meat-eater's head on a vegetarian's body.

1. After recording its position, workers protect each bone with sacking and plaster.

2. Back at the laboratory, technicians remove the plaster, along with any rock.

3. Palaeontologists study the bones and teeth to judge how the beast lived and moved.

4. Artists sketch details that would not show up in photographs of the bones.

Liquid resin

Pouring resin

5. Technicians make moulds, then fill them with resin.

6. This forms identical but much lighter replicas of the dinosaur's bones.

7. Finally, the replica bones are assembled on an armature (steel frame). This provides an impression of the dinosaur's vast bulk, but animated models give a better idea of how the creature looked.

Thin cables help support parts of the skeleton.

Welding armature together

Armature supports bones

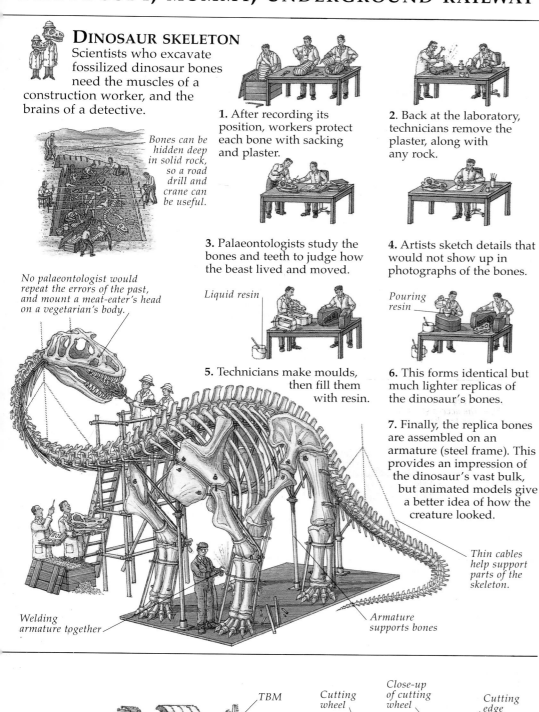

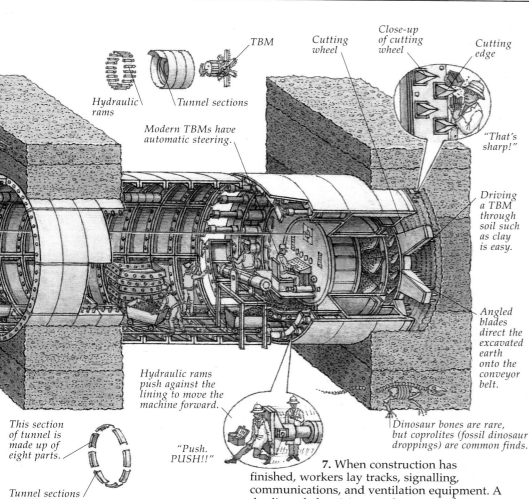

TBM

Cutting wheel

Close-up of cutting wheel

Cutting edge

Hydraulic rams

Tunnel sections

Modern TBMs have automatic steering.

"That's sharp!"

Driving a TBM through soil such as clay is easy.

Angled blades direct the excavated earth onto the conveyor belt.

Hydraulic rams push against the lining to move the machine forward.

"Push. PUSH!!"

This section of tunnel is made up of eight parts.

Tunnel sections bolt together. Assembling each ring from segments takes 15-30 minutes.

Dinosaur bones are rare, but coprolites (fossil dinosaur droppings) are common finds.

7. When construction has finished, workers lay tracks, signalling, communications, and ventilation equipment. A duplicated electricity supply ensures that a power failure never leaves stations and trains in darkness.

GAS

Gas is extracted by a long drill pipe 2,800 m (9,200 ft) under the sea bed. A drill pipe this long is as bendy as an earthworm.

1. The platform drills deep holes through solid undersea rock to reach gas reserves.

2. Turning the long pipe rotates the drill bit to cut a deeper hole.

Drilling platform

Gas and mud flow up the pipe from the drill site.

"Intelligent pig" checks the pipe for flaws.

Wells fan out as they go deeper.

Pipeline comes ashore

Rotating bits on the end of the drill pipe cut away the rock.

3. Once the gas comes ashore it flows to a refinery for processing.

4. The refinery removes poisonous hydrogen sulphide from the gas.

Seven huge tanks purify the gas.

The gas is dried here.

A tank stores sulphur products removed from the gas.

5. Chilling the gas condenses water. Removing the water dries out the gas.

The pure, dry gas is tested for quality here.

6. Gas has no smell, so the refinery adds one to warn consumers of leaks.

Huge tanks store the gas at the refinery until it is ready to be distributed.

7. Pumps move gas from the refinery to regional distribution centres.

8. The regional distribution centres reduce the pressure of the gas and store some in drum-shaped holders.

Computer programs help controllers pump the right amount of gas to consumers.

"The gas you burn for heating or cooking formed more than one million years ago!"

Distribution centre

Gas holder

Special sniffer vans patrol the streets to detect gas leaks before they can become a fire or explosion hazard.

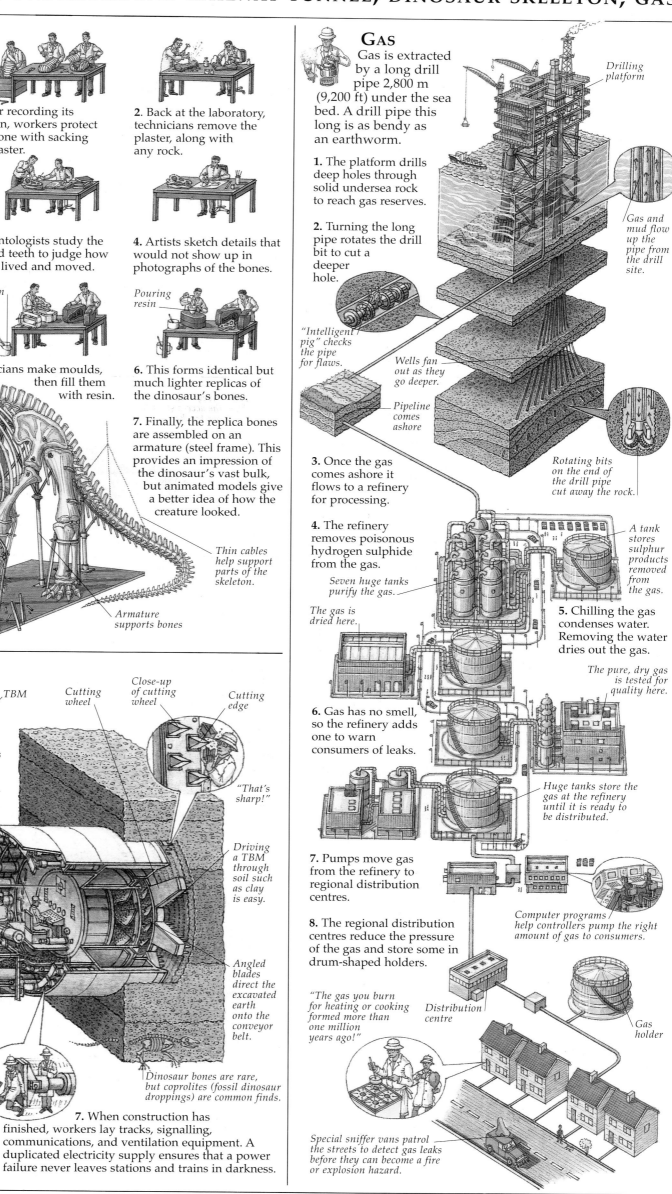

INDEX

A

advertising, 28
airliner, 18, 19
aluminium foil, 20
Apollo spacecraft, 12
armour, 16

B

body (car), 16-17, 22
Boeing 777, 18, 19
bottle (plastic), 17
brick, 24, 25
bridge (suspension), 10, 11
building
    cathedral, 24, 25
    tower block, 26, 27
    wooden house, 6, 7

C

cabin (airliner), 19
cables (bridge), 10
caissons, 10
car, 16, 17
    racing car, 22, 23
cathedral, 24, 25
charcoal, 24
chlorine, 17
chocolate bar, 26
clay, 24
clothing
    racing driver's, 23
    space suit, 12, 13
cockpit (airliner), 18
cocoa beans, 26
coin, 16, 17
colour printing, 28
command module, 12
compact disc, 8, 9
computer
    flight control system, 18
    laptop, 28
    newspaper, 28
    racing car, 22
    rocket, 13
computer design
    airliner, 18
    racing car, 22, 23
cows, 6

D

dental prostheses, 27
diamond ring, 9
dinosaur skeleton, 31
doughnut, 7
drill pipe, 31
drilling plaform, 31
drinking water, 17

E

Egyptian mummy, 30
electricity, 20, 21
energy supply
    gas, 31
    electricity, 20, 21
engines
    airliner, 18
    racing car, 22
    rocket, 13, 15
escape tower, 12
Extravehicular Mobility Unit, 12, 13

F

false teeth, 27
filtration (water), 17
flocculation tank, 17
fly-by-wire aircraft, 18
foundations
    bridge, 10
    cathedral, 24
    house, 6
    tower block, 26
fuel
    airliner, 19
    racing car, 22
    rocket, 15
fuselage (airliner), 19

G

gas, 31
glues, 6
Great Fire of London, 25
gunpowder, 24

H

house (wooden), 6, 7
Humber Bridge, 11

I

injection moulding, 9
injection blow moulding, 17

J

jewellery, 9
journalists, 28

L

lasers, 8, 30
lavatories (airliner), 19
lead roof, 25
locomotive (steam), 8, 9
Lunar Module, 12, 13
Lunar Roving Vehicle, 14

M

matches, 8, 9
milk, 6, 7
milking machine, 6
mint, 16
Moon landing, 12, 14
mummy, 30

N

nail, 26
news agency, 28
news reporting, 28
newspaper, 28, 29
newsprint, 29
nuclear chain reaction, 20
nuclear power, 20, 21

O

organ (pipe), 21

P

palaeontologists, 31
paper, 20, 21, 29
pasteurization, 7
photocopy, 30
pipe organ, 21
pit stop, 23
plastic, 17, 19
plywood, 6
power station (nuclear), 20, 21
printing plate, 28
printing press, 28, 29

R

racing car, 22, 23
refinery (gas), 31
reservoir, 17
ring (diamond), 9
road deck (bridge), 11
robots
    car plant, 16
    milking, 6

S

St Paul's Cathedral, 25
saltpetre, 24
Saturn V rocket, 12–15
soap, 20
space suit, 12, 13
spoilers, 23
steam locomotive, 8, 9
sulphur, 24
suspension (car), 22
suspension bridge, 10, 11

T

tanker (milk), 6
tap water, 17
teeth (false), 27
tinder box, 8
tower block, 26, 27
towers (bridge), 10
training shoe, 25
transformers, 21
tunnel, 30, 31
tunnel-boring machine, 30

U

underground tunnel, 30, 31
uranium, 20

V

vaults, 25
Vehicle Assembly Building, 15
veneers, 6

W

Walker, John, 8
walls
    tower block, 27
    wooden house, 7
water (drinking), 17
wig, 24
wind tunnel, 18, 23
wing (airliner), 18, 19
wood pulp, 20
World War I, 26

ACKNOWLEDGMENTS

Dorling Kindersley would like to thank the following for helping with this book:

Design: Joanne Earl, Ann Cannings

Editorial: Francesca Baines, Shirin Patel, Miranda Smith, Angela Koo, Nancy Jones, Nigel Ritchie

Index: Chris Bernstein

Research: Brian Sims at News International Newspapers Ltd; Man Roland Druckmaschinen; London Brick Company; Peter Middleton at Peter Middleton Associates; Kay Grinter at Kennedy Space Center; Neil Marshall at the Humber Bridge Board; Dunkin' Donuts; National Dairy Council; Dara McDonough at Disctronics Europe Ltd; De Beers; Jack Ogden at the National Association of Goldsmiths; Kevin Crowley at Rexam Foil and Paper Ltd; Gordon Grieve at Wig Creations; Alistair Watkins, Federation Internationale de l'Automobile; and Hugh Robertson at the London Transport Museum.